MW00947415

Mortage Terms

Financial Education Is Your Best Investment

Published March 02, 2020

Revision 2.2

Financial Terms Dictionary

Copyright And Trademark Notices

Limits of Liability and Disclaimer of Warranties

The materials in this book are provided "as is" and without warranties of any kind either express or implied. The Author disclaims all warranties, express or implied, including, but not limited to, implied warranties of merchantability and fitness for a particular purpose.

The Author does not warrant that defects will be corrected, or that that the site or the server that makes this eBook available are free of viruses or other harmful components. The Author does not warrant or make any representations regarding the use or the results of the use of the materials in this book in terms of their correctness, accuracy, reliability, or otherwise. Applicable law may not allow the exclusion of implied warranties, so the above exclusion may not apply to you.

Under no circumstances, including, but not limited to, negligence, shall the Author be liable for any special or consequential damages that result from the use of, or the inability to use this eBook, even if the Author or his authorized representative has been advised of the possibility of such damages.

Applicable law may not allow the limitation or exclusion of liability or incidental or consequential damages, so the above limitation or exclusion may not apply to you. In no event shall the Author's total liability to you for all damages, losses, and causes of action (whether in contract, tort, including but not limited to, negligence or otherwise) exceed the amount paid by you, if any, for this eBook.

Facts and information are believed to be accurate at the time they were placed in this book. All data provided in this book is to be used for information purposes only. The information contained within is not intended to provide specific legal, financial or tax advice, or any other advice whatsoever, for any individual or company and should not be relied upon in that regard. The services described are only offered in jurisdictions where they may be legally offered. Information provided is not all-inclusive and is limited to information that is made available and such information should not be relied upon as all-inclusive or accurate.

You are advised to do your own due diligence when it comes to making business decisions and should use caution and seek the advice of qualified professionals. You should check with your accountant, lawyer, or professional advisor, before acting on this or any information. You may not consider any examples, documents, or other content in this eBook or otherwise provided by the Author to be the equivalent of professional advice.

The Author assumes no responsibility for any losses or damages resulting from your use of any link, information, or opportunity contained in this book or within any other information disclosed by the author in any form whatsoever.

About the Author

Thomas Herold is a successful entrepreneur, mediator, author, and personal development coach. He published over 35 books with over 200,000 copies distributed worldwide and the founder of seven online businesses.

For over ten years Thomas Herold has studied the monetary system and has experienced some profound insights on how money and wealth are related. After three years of successful investing in silver, he released 'Building Wealth with Silver - How to Profit From The Biggest Wealth Transfer in History' in 2012. One of the first books that illustrate in a remarkable, simple way the monetary system and its consequences.

He is the founder and CEO of the 'Financial Terms Dictionary' book series and website, which explains in detail and comprehensive form over 1000 financial terms. In his financial book series, he informs in detail and with practical examples all aspects of the financial sector. His educational materials are designed to help people get started with financial education.

In his 2018 released book 'The Money Deception', Mr. Herold provides the most sophisticated insight and shocking details about the current monetary system. Never before has the massive manipulation of money caused so much economic inequality in the world. In spite of these frightening facts, 'The Money Deception' also provides remarkable and simple solutions to create abundance for all people, and it's a must-read if you want to survive the global monetary transformation that's underway right now.

In 2019 he released an entirely new financial book series explaining in detail and with practical examples over 1000 financial terms. The 'Herold Financial IQ Series' contains currently of 16 titles covering every category of the financial market.

His latest book "High Credit Score Secrets" offers the most effective strategies to boost the average credit score from as low as 450 points to over 810. It teaches the tactics to build excellent credit, repair credit, monitor credit and how to guard that good score for a lifetime. It reached bestseller status in 2020 in three categories.

For more information please visit the author's websites:

High Credit Score Secrets - The Smart Raise & Repair Guide to Excellent Credit
https://highcreditscoresecrets.com

The Money Deception - What Banks & Government Don't Want You to Know
https://www.moneydeception.com

The Herold Financial IQ Series - Financial Education Is Your Best Investment
https://www.financial-dictionary.com

The Online Financial Dictionary - Over 1000 Terms Explained
https://www.financial-dictionary.info

Please Leave Your Review on Amazon

This book and the Financial IQ Series are self-published and the author does not have a contract with one of the five largest publishers, which are able to support the author's work with advertising. If you like this book, please consider leaving a solid 4 or 5-star review on Amazon.

Herold Financial IQ Series on Amazon

Table Of Contents

Absorption Rate

Absorption rate is a term used in real estate. It represents the speed with which homes available in a real estate market are sold in a certain amount of time. Real estate professionals figure out this absorption rate by taking the number of houses that are available and dividing this by the average number of sales in a month. The result provides a useful number. It is the total number of months it will require before all of the homes on the market are sold.

It is important to note that this absorption rate does not consider any supplies of other houses that enter the real estate market. As such it is a snapshot of a fixed moment in time. Higher absorption rates will usually signify that the numbers of available houses will decrease quickly. This means that a homeowner would likely sell his or her house in a shorter time frame.

In historical context, when the rates of absorption rose over 20%, this has meant that the market was ideal for sellers. Homes would sell fast. When the absorption rate proved to be lower than 15%, this means that a buyer's market is in effect. Buyers are being pickier. This slows down the rate at which homes are being sold.

The absorption rate is easier to understand by looking at an example. In this scenario, a given city has 2,000 houses that are up for sale. If buyers came into the market and bought up 200 homes each month, then the home supply would be depleted in 10 months. This is simply figured by dividing the 2,000 houses by 200 homes bought each month.

When buyers purchase the 200 houses from the 2,000 houses total, it means the rate of absorption equals 10%. This number is derived by taking the 200 houses buyers purchase every month and dividing it by the total 2,000 houses for sale. It would mean that the market is optimal for buyers. Any homeowner who was hoping to sell a house would be aware that the market should half sell out over a period of five months.

There are a number of different individuals who work with this important figure. Real estate industry professionals are most interested in the number. Real estate brokers would put this number to use when they price houses. If a market showed signs of lower rates of absorption, the agents might have no choice but to lower the listing price in order to attract a buyer. In the opposite case, the market might exhibit a higher rate. This would allow the realtor to raise the home price without eliminating demand on the property.

Home builders also look at these absorption rates when they are thinking about building new properties. A higher rate is often interpreted by the construction industry as an optimal time to begin building new houses. When the conditions on the market show higher absorption, it means demand can likely support them developing additional properties. The opposite is true if there is less absorption. This tells them that demand is lower. Construction may pause in efforts to build new houses.

A last group that carefully studies the rates of absorption are the property appraisers. They think about these rates when they are considering the total value of a given property. In 2009, new appraisal rules came into effect. These mandated that every home value appraisal connected with a home loan had to take into account the active rate of absorption. The reasoning behind this was that home values should be less in times where lower absorption resulted in fewer and more drawn out sales at lower prices.

Adjustable Rate Mortgage (ARM)

Adjustable Rate Mortgages, also known by their acronym ARM's, are those mortgages whose interest rates change from time to time. These changes commonly occur based on an index. As a result of changing interest rates, payments will rise and fall along with them.

Adjustable Rate Mortgages involve a number of different elements. These include margins, indexes, discounts, negative amortization, caps on payments and rates, recalculating of your loan, and payment options. When considering an adjustable rate mortgage, you should always understand both the most that your monthly payments might go up, as well as your ability to make these higher payments in the future.

Initial payments and rates are important to understand with these ARM's. They stay in effect for only certain time frames that run from merely a month to as long as five years or longer. With some of these ARM's, these initial payments and rates will vary tremendously from those that are in effect later in the life of the loan. Your payments and rates can change significantly even when interest rates remain level. A way to determine how much this will vary on a particular ARM loan is to compare the annual percentage rate and the initial rate. Should this APR prove to be much greater than the initial rate, then likely the payments and rates will similarly turn out to be significantly greater when the loan adjusts.

It is important to understand that the majority of Adjustable Rate Mortgages' monthly payments and interest rates will vary by the month, the quarter, the year, the three year period, and the five year time frame. The time between these changes in rate is referred to as the adjustment period. Loans that feature one year periods are called one year ARM's, as an example.

These Adjustable Rate Mortgages' interest rates are comprised of two portions of index and margin. The index actually follows interest rates themselves. Your payments are impacted by limits on how far the rate can rise or fall. As the index rises, so will your interest rates and payments generally. As the index declines, your monthly payments could similarly fall, assuming that your ARM is one that adjusts down. ARM rates can be based on a number of different indexes, including LIBOR the London Interbank Offered rate, COFI the Cost of Funds Index, and a CMT one year constant maturity Treasury security. Other lenders use their own proprietary model.

Margin proves to be the premium to the rate that a lender itself adds. This is commonly a couple of percentage points that are added directly to the index rate amount. These amounts vary from one lender to the next, and are commonly fixed during the loan term. The fully indexed rate is comprised of index plus margin. When the loan's initial rate turns out to be lower than the fully indexed rate, this is referred to as a discounted index rate. So an index that sat at five percent and had a three percent margin tacked on would be a fully indexed rate of eight percent.

Affidavit

An Affidavit is a declaration in writing which includes a sworn oath or positive confirmation that written contents are factual and true. These declarations and statements could be made related to court cases. They also could be made to support an important document as with mortgage applications or tax returns.

Though many people may not be aware of it, a great number of forms prove to be affidavits. This is because they have a line that states the individuals have filled in the form to the best of their knowledge. The line must also mention that deliberately entering information that is incorrect will lead to perjury charges. If a person is found guilty of perjury charges, it can lead to significant time spent in jail.

The word affidavit is originally taken from the Latin. The Latin roots signifies that individuals have pledged their faith with complete knowledge of the law. It is interesting that affidavits are always voluntarily undertaken documents. This means that no parties in a court case are able to make a person give such statement under oath. Courts can force individuals to give deposition accounts. Depositions differ from an affidavit. They may both be statements that are written, but depositions will be cross examined in a court.

Affidavits must involve knowledge that is personally known by the individual who declares them. This means that persons who do not include information of which they were unaware will not be punished or deemed to be in perjury. Personal knowledge can cover a person's opinion too. In such cases, the statement must be unequivocally stated to be opinion instead of a known fact. Any individual is allowed to provide an affidavit if he or she maintains the necessary mental ability to comprehend how serious the oath given actually is. This is why guardians of mentally ill patients are able to provide such an affidavit on their behalf.

These documents are generally formally witnessed by a qualified official such as a notary public or an account clerk. Notaries are agents who receive a small fee in exchange for witnessing the signing of legal documents for individuals, as with mortgage forms or real estate transactions. This witness signing the document means that the person pledges that the information is accurate and realizes how important this oath is. Documents like these can be utilized in court as evidence. They can also be submitted alongside supporting materials with various kinds of transactions, including for social services.

Individuals who sign affidavits should be extremely careful that they read the documents several times, especially if another individual is recording them. This is because the documents are oaths which are legally binding. The statements contained within must be correctly and clearly related. When the signor recognizes errors in the document, as with facts on a mortgage application, these need to be corrected in advance of signing. This is more important than the inconvenience it will cause the officials who have written down the information and who are witnessing the signing and oath that accompanies it.

Amortization

The word amortization is one that is commonly utilized by financial officers of corporations and accountants. They utilize it when they are working with time concepts and how they relate to financial statements of accounts. You typically hear this word employed when you are figuring up loan calculations, or when you are determining interest payments.

The concept of amortization possesses a lengthy history and it is currently employed in numerous different segments of finance. The word itself descends from Middle English. Here amortisen meant to "alienate" or "kill" something. This derivation itself comes from the Latin admortire that signified "plus death." It is loosely related to the derivation of the word mortgage, as well.

This accounting principle is much like depreciation that diminishes a liability or asset's value over a given period of time through payments. It covers the practical life span of a tangible asset. With liabilities, it includes a pre-set amount of time over which money is paid back. Like this, a certain amount of money is set aside for the loan repayment over its lifetime.

Even though depreciation is similar to amortization, they are not the same concepts. The main difference between them lies in what they cover. While depreciation is most commonly employed to describe physical assets like property, vehicles, or buildings, amortization instead covers intangibles such as product development, copyrights, or patents. Where liabilities are concerned, it relates to income in the future that will be paid out over a given amount of time. Depreciation is instead a lost income over a time period.

Several different kinds of amortization are presently in use. This varies with the accounting method that is practiced. Business amortization deals with borrowed funds and loans and the paying of particular amounts in different time frames. When used as amortization analysis, this is the means of cost execution analysis for a given group of operations. Where tax law is concerned, amortization pertains to the interest amount that is paid over a given span of time relevant to payments and tax rates.

Amortization can also be employed with regards to zoning rules and regulations, since it conveys a property owner's time for relocating as a result of zoning guidelines and pre-existing use. Another variation is used as negative amortization. This pertains specifically to increasing loan amounts that result from total interest due not being paid up at the appropriate time.

Amortization can also be employed over a widely ranging time frame. It could cover only a year or extend to as many as forty years. This depends on the kind of loan or asset utilized. Some examples include building loans that span over as many as forty years and car loans that commonly span over merely four to five years. Asset examples would be patent right expenses that commonly are spread out over seventeen years.

Annual Percentage Rate (APR)

The annual percentage rate, or APR, is the actual interest rate that a loan charges each year. This single percentage number is truthfully used to represent the literal annual expense of using money over the life span of a given loan. Annual percentage rate not only covers interest charged, but can also be comprised of extra costs or fees that are attached to a given loan transaction.

Credit cards and loans commonly offer differing explanations for transaction fees, the structure of their interest rates, and any late fees that are assessed. The annual percentage rate provides an easy to understand formula for expressing to borrowers the real and actual percentage number of fees and interest so that they can measure these up against the rates that other possible lenders will charge them.

Annual percentage rate can include many different elements besides interest. With a nominal APR, it simply involves the rate of a given payment period multiplied out to the exact numbers of payment periods existing in a year. The effective APR is often referred to as the mathematically true rate of interest for a given year. Effective APR's are commonly the fees charged plus the rate of compound interest.

On a home mortgage, effective annual percentage rates could factor in Private Mortgage Insurance, discount points, and even processing costs. Some hidden fees do not make their ways into an effective APR number. Because of this, you should always read the fine print surrounding an APR and the costs associated with a mortgage or loan. As an example of how an effective APR can be deceptive with mortgages, the one time fees that are charged in the front of a mortgage are commonly assumed to be divided over a loan's long repayment period. If you only utilize the loan for a short time frame, then the APR number will be thrown off by this. An effective APR on a mortgage might look lower than it actually is when the loan will be paid off significantly earlier than the term of the loan.

The government created the concept of annual percentage rate to stop loan companies and credit cards issuers from deceiving consumers with fancy expressions of interest charges and fees. The law requires that all loan issuers and credit card companies have to demonstrate this annual percentage rate to all customers. This is so the consumers will obtain a fair comprehension of the true rates that are associated with their particular transactions. While credit card companies are in fact permitted to promote their monthly basis of interest rates, they still have to clearly show the actual annual percentage rate to their customers in advance of a contract or agreement being signed by the consumer.

Annual percentage rate is sometimes confused with annual percentage yield. This can be vastly different from the APR. Annual percentage yield includes calculations of compounded interest in its numbers.

Annual Percentage Yield (APY)

APY describes the amount of compound interest which individuals or businesses will earn in a given year (or longer time period). Investments in money market accounts, savings accounts, and CD Certificates of Deposit all pay out such interest. It is the annual percentage yield that demonstrates precisely the amount in interest individuals will receive. This is helpful for people or businesses trying to ascertain which investments and banks offer superior returns by comparing and contrasting their real yields. In general, higher Annual Percentage Yields are better to have (unless one is comparing interest on credit card debts).

This APY is practical to understand and measure simply because it considers compound interest and the miracle of compounding within any account. Simple interest rates do not do this. Compounding is simply earning interest on interest that has already accrued and been paid. It signifies that individuals are gaining a greater amount in interest than the corresponding interest rate literally indicates.

It is always a good idea to consider a real world example for clarification purposes. If Fred deposits $10,000 into a particular savings account that provides a two percent yearly interest rate, then at the end of that first year Fred will have $10,200. This assumes that the interest is paid one time per year. If the bank were to figure up and pay out the interest on a daily basis, it would increase the amount to $10,202. The extra $2 may seem small, but given a longer time frame of from 10 to 30 years, this amount can add up, particularly if larger deposits are involved.

APY should never be confused with APR. They have some similarities, but APR does not consider compounding. It is once again a simpler means of computing interest. Credit card loans are an area where it is important to understand the differences between annual percentage rate and annual percentage yield. When people carry a balance, they will be paying higher APY's then the APR the firm actually quotes. This is because interest is assessed monthly, which means that interest on the interest will be computed on each following month.

The key to obtaining a better APY on investments and savings accounts lies in getting as frequent a compounding period as possible. Quarterly compounding is better than annually, yet daily is the most superior form of compounding possible. This means that as individuals are looking to increase their APY's personally, it is important to have the money compounding as frequently as they can practically achieve.

When two CD Certificates of Deposit pay out the same rate, it is best to select that one which actually pays out both more frequently and also boasts the greater APY. With CD's, the interest payments become automatically reinvested. More frequent reinvestment is always better. This will help any individual or business to earn a greater amount of interest on the interest payments already earned and paid out.

Calculating the annual percentage yield is not an easy task. Business calculators as well as computer algorithms mostly do it for people nowadays. The simplest way to find the APY for a given account is to plug in the information including the initial deposit, compounding frequency period, interest rate, and amount of overall time for the period considered. These smart calculators will then tell you both the effective annual percentage yield as well as the ending balance on the hypothetical account at the end of the given time period.

Appraisal

Appraisals are professionally done estimates of a property's real value. These are conducted by appraisers. Many things can have an appraisal done on them, including smaller items like artwork or jewelry, as well as larger things like businesses, commercial buildings, or homes.

Appraisals are commonly required before many different transactions can be performed. In advance of getting a house, piece of jewelry, or an artwork insured, appraisals must be performed. Homes and offices have to be appraised for insurance, loans, and tax purposes. Appraisals ensure that these loans and insurance policies are comparable to the property's tangible market value.

Several different types of appraisals can be performed. Real property appraisal involves properly estimating Real Estate value. Personal property appraisal involves determining the worth of valuable individual objects like expensive china, jewelry, pottery, artwork, heirlooms, and antiques. Mass appraisals merge real property and personal property appraisals into a single appraisal. Business value appraisals consider all of the valuable tangible and intangible assets that a business owns, including logos, services, equipment, property, inventory, other assets and goodwill.

Perhaps the most commonly used type of appraisal is a home appraisal. Home appraisals prove to be professionally done surveys of a house to come up with an opinion or estimate of the home's value on the market. These kinds of appraisals are usually performed for banks that are considering the approval of a loan for a person purchasing a home. Such home appraisals turn out to be detailed reports. These cover many things including the home's neighborhood, the house's condition, how rapidly area houses sell, and what comparable houses actually sell for at the time.

Such a home appraisal could similarly be done for a replacement value for insurance purposes or as a sales comparison in marketing a home, as well. Cost and replacement appraisals determine what the actual cost to completely replace your home would be if something destroyed the house. This type of appraisal is most often employed for new houses. Sales comparison appraisals more often examine various additional properties within your house's neighborhood to determine at what price they are presently selling. The appraiser will then determine how such houses compare and contrast against your particular home.

Home appraisals commonly cost in the range of from $300 to $500 when people decide to order one done themselves. Such appraisals are not often accepted by banks. They will want to have their own contracted appraiser make the estimate in order to get a more independent number that they trust.

Home appraisers are always licensed by the state in which they operate. The highest of ethical standards are demanded of them. Their sole purpose is to act as an independent third party who will give their truthful opinion of a home's market value. Appraisers are not supposed to be associated with any party that is involved in the selling of a home.

Appraised Value

Assessed Value

Assessed Value refers to the specific dollar value amount which a municipality assigns to a certain property. They do this for the purpose of determining the relevant taxes for the property and owner. These assessed valuations actually create a given residence's tax purpose value. They do this through considering inspections and any comparable home sales in the area. Once this is all completed, the municipal government will set a value on the home and then assess the due property taxes. The owner then receives the final bill for municipal taxes on the property. The assessment value is also called the ad valorem tax.

Most of the time, such Assessed Value proves to be less than the associated fair market value or appraisal value for the property in question. This assessment value is a number with very limited uses. It only applies to the relevant property tax in question.

The person who has the role for determining the Assessed Value turns out to be a government assessor. These individuals are typically assigned by particular taxing districts. It is true that every taxing jurisdiction maintains its own rules and procedures for determining the actual assessment value. Despite this, the general standards which they rely on are nearly identical.

The assessors are expected to make these valuations on a yearly basis. This is where the property tax bill comes from every year. Most years, the assessment value will not change. The Assessed Value is derived from the fair market value, of which they set a certain percentage. They consider a number of different elements in determining this. Chief among these are comparable property values, condition of the property, features of the house, total square footage and air conditioned square footage, and conditions in the market. A great number of such calculations prove to be derived from the computer models. These come from official real estate databases on regions and neighborhoods.

Besides such computer-based real estate data, the government assessors will do physical assessments onsite when necessary. Some states have exacting and specific requirements for the ways in which their government assessors have to visit the various properties which are being assessed in person. There are also rules regarding property owner objections to a set value. They can dispute the value on their given house and can ask for a reassessment visit. This is carried out in practice as a property second evaluation.

In the majority of states, the final numbers which the jurisdictions come up with represent a certain percentage of the fair market value for a given property. This assessed value ratio can range significantly from one state to another. It could in theory be as wide a variance as from 10 percent to 100 percent of the fair market value of the property in question. At only ten percent assessed value ratio, Mississippi boasts among the lowest ones in the United States. Coming in at a staggering 100 percent assessed value ratio is Massachusetts in the typically tax-heavy Northeast and New England regions.

Most states utilize a set property tax formula when determining their so-called millage rate. Millage rate refers to the actual tax rate compiled for the assessed value. This is the value times millage rate times assessment ratio equals the effective property tax. They are commonly described per $1,000. A single mill equates to $1 of tax for each $1,000.

The majority of the states also require a personal property tax to be levied. This comes from the assessed value of other forms of property. Personal property that has tax assessed on it includes cars, mobile homes, boats, and motorcycles.

Asset Protection

Asset Protection and planning refers to strategies and practices for protecting personal wealth. It happens through deliberate and involved planning processes that safeguard individuals' assets from the potential claims of any creditors. Both businesses and individuals alike can employ these specific techniques to reduce the ability of creditors to seize personal or business property within the legal boundaries of creditor debtor law.

What makes Asset Protection so powerful is that it is able to insulate a variety of assets and all legally. It does not require any of the shady or illegal activities inherent in concealing assets, illegal money transferring, bankruptcy fraud, or tax evasion. The asset experts will warn their clients that efficient protection of assets starts in advance of a liability, incident, or claim occurring. The reason is that it is generally over late to begin arranging such protection afterward. There are a wide variety of normal means for protecting such personal or business assets. Among the most popular are family limited partnerships, accounts receivable financing, and asset protection trusts.

In the heavily litigious society of the United States, Asset Protection involves protecting property from those who might win a judgment in court. There are a variety of lawsuits that could threaten a person's or business' assets. Among these are car accident claims, unintentional negligent acts, and even foreclosure on property lawsuits where the mortgage is no longer paid. The ultimate goal in Asset Protection is to take any nonexempt from creditors assets and move them to a position where they become exempt assets beyond the reach of any claims of the various creditors.

Asset Protection which an individual or business does when a lawsuit is already underway or even imminent to be filed will likely be reversed by the courts. This way they can seize the hidden assets that were deliberately transferred to protect them from an imminent court case judgment. This is the ultimate reason why effective protection of assets has to start well in advance of the first hints of litigious activity or creditor claims.

Two principal goals must be combined in order to effectively construct an efficient and ironclad Asset Protection plan. These include achieving both long term and short term goals and reaching estate planning goals. The financial goals component involves clearly understanding present and future income sources, the amount of resources needed for retirement, and any resources which will remain to leave to any heirs via estate planning. This helps people to come up with highly detailed financial plans.

After this has been done, individuals will want to examine carefully any present assets to decide if they are effectively exempted from any and all sundry creditors. The ones that are not should be clearly repositioned so that they are exempt. This also involves planning to position future assets so that they are similarly effectively protected.

The next step is to come up with a complete and all inclusive estate plan. It should encompass all forms of asset protection and relevant planning via advanced techniques of estate planning. Among these are irrevocable trusts for the individuals, their children, spouses, and beneficiaries as well as family limited liability companies.

The most common mistake that people or businesses make with this Asset Protection planning is waiting until it is too late to safeguard the assets. The other mistake is assuming that such planning can be done rapidly or as a short term fix for a longer term problem. Protecting assets is ultimately longer term planning that must be done carefully and ahead of potential creditor claims on assets or pending lawsuits.

Assumable Loan

An assumable loan is one that permits a home buyer to take over, or assume, a home seller's contract on their mortgage. This is not permitted by every mortgage lender in the place of a typical home purchase. Loans that do not have Due On Sale clauses, such as the majority of VA and FHA types of mortgages, can usually be assumed and are considered to be assumable loans.

Assumable home loans work in the following manner. A current home owner will simply transfer over his or her mortgage contract and obligations to a purchaser who is qualified to take over. In the past decades of the 1970's and 1980's, these types of mortgage note assumptions proved to be quite popular. Back then, they could be done without even having to obtain the mortgage lender's authorization. These days, the only types of mortgages that may be assumable loans without needing a lender's actual permission are those that are made by the FHA or VA.

Assumable loans provide opportunities for both buyers and sellers. It is often the case that a home buyer will not be able to secure a better rate for a new mortgage than that provided by an already existing mortgage. This could result from the negative credit history of the buyer in question or the conditions existing in the market place at the time. As existing interest rates rise, the appeal of non-existent lower rates on mortgages commonly pushes prospective home buyers to look out for assumable loans. Such a home buyer who secures an assumable loan then has the responsibility for the mortgage that the home seller previously carried.

The existing rates of the mortgage carry over for the buyer as if the person had made the original contract themselves. This assumable loan process also saves the buyer a number of the settlement costs that are incurred in making a new mortgage. This can be a substantial cost savings benefit.

Sellers similarly benefit from assumable loans. It is not uncommon for sellers to wish to be involved in the savings that buyers realize in the process of transferring over an assumable loan. Because of this, the two parties commonly share in the savings.

As an example, when the sale price of the home in question is greater than the amount owed on the mortgage itself, then the buyer will often have to put down a significant down payment, which goes straight to the home seller in this case. Otherwise, the buyer might have to get another mortgage to come up with the difference in amounts. A seller's principal benefit in participating in such an assumable loan transfer lies in having a good chance of getting a better price for the home.

Automated Underwriting

Automated underwriting proves to be one of the biggest changes that has come to the mortgage lending business in the last several years. The process uses computers to handle the process of underwriting mortgage loans. There are numerous benefits to the concept. Among them are lower closing costs, quicker loan approvals, fewer requirements for documentation, and approval for applications which human underwriters denied in the past.

Underwriting itself is the means whereby the underwriters approve or deny mortgage loans. They do this by considering the property, the ability to pay back the loan, and the credit worthiness of the individuals applying. For most of mortgage loan history, people exclusively handled these activities. In recent years, programs have demonstrated that computers are able to perform these jobs quicker, with greater accuracy, and generally better.

There are now automated underwriting systems that handle much of this work load. Both Freddie Mac and Fannie Mae have created their own such systems to evaluate mortgage loans. They are the two biggest investors in mortgages within the United States. Freddie Mac has a system called Loan Prospector. Fannie Mae developed Desktop Underwriter to perform these same functions. Both computer systems display their abilities via a predictive model. They take the specific mortgage applications and compute a quantitative risk factor for them.

Automated underwriting systems are easy to apply through. The lender or mortgage broker queries the applicant for information. He or she enters this data into the underwriting system. The system pulls a credit report to accompany it. The system next creates a Findings Report using the credit report and application information. The Findings Report reveals the determination on the loan application approval. It provides the list of documents that will be required in order to verify the data of the application.

Consumers benefit from these systems. The approvals they issue represent binding commitments from either Freddie Mac or Fannie Mae. If the information put in is correct and can be documented, then the consumers can enjoy the confidence of knowing that their loan will be issued.

Borrowers no longer have to come up with voluminous amounts of application documents and complete major paperwork thanks to these systems. The new automated underwriting systems commonly only require a single pay stub instead of the two months that human underwriters typically wanted.

Approval time spans are significantly shorter now with these computers. The Findings Report appears in only minutes after the lender enters the information into the system. Less documentation also means that the time frames are reduced.

Consumers receive the benefit of the savings from these systems. Appraisal fees are typically $100 less. Credit report costs come down by $50 or more. Loan origination fees may be less as well.

The greatest single benefit of the new systems is that with automated underwriting, consumers who used to be refused loans are many times approved now. Consumers with excellent credit but fewer down payment resources especially benefit from this system. In the past they would not have been approved, but the system model assigns less importance to the full down payment amount that human underwriters did.

One helpful characteristic of these automated underwriting systems revolves around property identification. Human underwriters often required the property for which they were applying for a mortgage to be stated on the application. The new systems do not have such a requirement. This benefits consumers who are still shopping for a house. Once they are approved by the system, they gain a powerful tool for negotiating deals with the sellers of properties.

Balloon Loan

A balloon loan is a kind of loan that does not divide its payments up evenly throughout the life of the loan. These kinds of loans are not fully amortized over the loan's term. As a result of this, one time balloon payments are mandatory at the end of the loan's time frame in order to pay off the loan's remaining principal balance.

Balloon loans have their advantages. They are often appealing to you if you are a short term borrower. This is because balloon loans commonly come with an interest rate that is lower than the interest rate of a longer term loan. These lower interest rates provide a benefit of extremely low interest payments. This leads to not only lower payments throughout the loan, but also incredibly low outlays of capital in the life span of the loan. Because the majority of the loan repayment is put off until the loan payment period's conclusion, a borrower gains great flexibility in using the capital that is freed up for the term of the loan.

The downsides to these balloon loans only surface when the borrower lacks discipline or falls victim to higher interest rates later on. If a borrower does not possess focused and consistent discipline in getting ready for the large last payment, then the individual may run into trouble at the end of the loan. This is because substantial payments along the way are not being collected. Besides this, if a borrower will be forced to engage in refinancing towards the end, then the borrower may suffer from a higher interest rate on the balloon payment that is rolled forward.

Some balloon loans also include a higher interest rate reset feature later in the life of the loan. This further exposes a borrower to the risk of higher interest rates. This is common with five year types of balloon mortgages. When a reset of the interest rate feature is present at the conclusion of the five year period, then the interest rate will be adjusted to the current rates. The amortization schedule will then be recalculated dependent on a final term of the loan. Balloon options that do not include these reset options, and many that do reset, generally encourage the loan holder to sell the property in advance of the conclusion of the original term of the loan. Otherwise, many borrowers will simply choose to refinance the loan before this point arrives.

The reasons that you might choose to get a balloon loan are several. A person who does not plan to hold onto a house or property for a long period of time would benefit from such a loan arrangement. This individual would plan to resell the house in advance of the loan expiration. Another reason for taking a balloon loan is in a refinancing. Finally, if a person anticipates a significant cash settlement or lump sum award, then they might take on a balloon loan. Commercial property owners often like balloon loans for the purchase of commercial properties as well.

Balloon loans are sometimes called balloon notes or bullet loans.

Bankruptcy

Bankruptcy is a term that refers to the elimination or restructuring of a person or company's debt. Three principal different types of bankruptcy filing are available. These are the personal bankruptcy options of Chapter 7 and Chapter 13 filings, and the business bankruptcy restructuring option of Chapter 11.

Individuals avail themselves of Chapter 7 or Chapter 13 bankruptcy filings when their financial situations warrant significant help. With a Chapter 7 filing, all of an individual's debt is erased through discharge. This provides a new start for the debtor. Due to changes in laws made back in October 2005, not every person is able to obtain this type of total debt relief any longer. As a result of this new bankruptcy law, a means test came into being that prospective bankruptcy filers must successfully pass if they are to prove eligibility for this kind of bankruptcy relief.

The net effect of this new test is that consumers find it much more difficult to qualify for total debt elimination under Chapter 7. Besides the means test, the cost of bankruptcy attorneys has now risen dramatically by upwards of a hundred percent as a result of the new laws. Before these laws went into effect, Chapter 7 filings represented around seventy percent of all personal filings for bankruptcy. Chapter 7 offered the individual the advantage of simply walking away from debts that they might be capable of paying back with sufficient time and some interest rate help.

Chapter 13 Bankruptcy filings prove to be much like debt restructuring procedures. In these proceedings, a person's creditors are made to agree to the repayment of principal and zero interest on debts over a longer span of time. The individual gets to keep all of her or his assets in this form of filing. The most common motivation for Chapter 13 proves to be a desire to stop a foreclosure on a home. Individuals are able to achieve this by halting foreclosure proceedings and catch up on back mortgage payments. Once a court examines the debtor's budget, it will sign off on the plan for repayment proposed by the person. Depending on the level of an individual's income, he or she may have no choice but to file a Chapter 13 filling, as a result to the 2005 law changes.

Companies and corporations that are in financial distress may avail themselves of bankruptcy protection as well. Chapter 11 allows for such businesses to have protection from their creditors while they restructure their debt. Some individuals who have a higher income level will take advantage of this form of filing as well, since it does not place income restrictions on the entity filing. It has been instrumental in saving many large and well known companies over the years, including K-Mart, that actually emerged strong enough from the Chapter 11 bankruptcy to buy out higher end rival Sears afterward.

Blanket Loans

Blanket loans are those which cover multiple properties or parcels of land. They handle the costs for or can be secured by more than a single piece of real estate. These are most typically employed by commercial land developers or investors. For individual consumers, they can be utilized as a type of bridge between new and old properties and mortgages. For these consumers, such a blanket loan will make it possible to pay for both mortgages until the owner reaches the point of selling the old property.

The feature that makes these mortgages most useful for developers is their release clause. These permit the borrowers to sell a single or even several pieces of real estate without the need of being forced to refinance the mortgage. This makes them significantly different from traditional mortgages. Normal mortgages make borrowers completely pay down their loan balance before they can sell the property which secures them.

For developers of residential properties, they find these blanket loans particularly helpful. They employ them to pay for large tracts of land on which they will build. When it is time for the loan to fund, it becomes secured by the full piece of property. The developer is allowed to subdivide his property and sell it in individual lots. For part of the security to be released, the developer must utilize some of the sale proceeds to pay down part of the loan.

This is helpful when builders are constructing subdivisions. Such a developer could put the blanket loan to use to buy the consecutive pieces of land while they are available. The developer would then be able to subdivide the total land into specific lots for building houses. With each home that he finishes and sells, the property becomes detached from the blanket loan without the financing having to be disrupted on the remainder of the development project.

Consumers also find these types of blanket loans helpful in making it possible to transition from the sale of their current home to the building or buying of the new house. This makes much more sense than having two concurrent mortgages or obtaining a more costly short term bridge loan. It can also help them so that they do not have to sell the property early and move into a rental while they look for a property to purchase.

These kinds of blanket loans are often governed by a contingency clause. These clauses detail that the newly purchased house and its mortgage will not close until the person is able to sell the existing home. The problem with such a contingency clause is that they have limited time frames on them. They may force a borrower into selling the home in a panic in order to meet the clause expiration date. This can lead to a lower selling price or disadvantageous terms on the sale.

Blanket loans get around such a dilemma by providing the borrowers with an extended period of time in the clause to sell their old house. Sometimes they are arranged as interest payment only loans for a full 12 months before amortizing starts. This gives the seller a sufficient time period to sell the house for a good price and reduces the overall burden of the mortgage at the same time.

The main downside to blanket loans for individuals is that they are significantly harder to find since the real estate crash and Great Recession of 2009. Their advantages include both flexibility and efficiency in financing. For an individual consumer, this means a single mortgage payment rather than two. Developers do not have to worry about constantly refinancing their property debt as they sell off parts of the property. Should a developer default on his loan, the bank simply assumes control of all remaining property which secures the loan.

Bridge Loan

A bridge loan is a temporary short term loan whose purpose is to help a home owner to afford to buy a new house before they are able to sell their present house. They might do this to avoid having to move into a rental in between houses. The home buyer's existing house secure these loans. The money that comes from these loans is utilized to purchase the house into which the buyers are moving.

A bridge loan can be more popular in real estate markets which favor the buyer, or a buyer's market. The home owner may find it easier to buy a new house than to sell his or her existing one in these cases. This means that the buyers will have to come up with the down payment through either these types of loans or by using a home equity loan. Home equity loans can be less costly than bridge loans are.

A bridge loan will offer some borrowers greater advantages. Besides this, a great number of lenders will refuse to make a home equity loan on a house that is already up for sale. The best thing is to compare the advantages of the two different kinds of loan in order to decide which works best for a given buyer's unique scenario before he or she puts in an offer on another house.

Bridge loans do not always involve credit score minimums and set debt to income ratios. It depends on the lender and the underwriting process that is involved. Instead approvals are more often granted based on whether such underwriting makes sense to the loan officer and lender. There would be stricter guidelines on the part of the loan that pertains to the new house and its long term mortgage.

There are lenders who will make conforming loans and not consider the bridge loans' payments when qualifying the borrower for the new mortgage. In other cases the borrowers become qualified to purchase the new house by combining the present loan payment with the additional mortgage payment on the new house.

A great number of lenders will qualify the borrowers on two payments for a variety of reasons. They understand that the majority of buyers already have a current first mortgage on the home which they own. Banks also know that buyers would probably close on the new house they are buying before they sell their present home. Most importantly, banks are aware that home buyers in this scenario will own two different houses, even if for a short time frame. Qualifying on a bridge loan based on two payments requires a greater income or a lower payment on one of the houses.

With conforming loans, banks and lenders can find more room to work with a greater debt to income ratio. They can do this by using one of the automated mortgage underwriting programs with Freddie Mae or Fannie Mac. In general with jumbo loans, the restrictions are greater. The majority of lenders will limit the borrower to a maximum of 50% debt to income ratio.

Bubble

In economic terms, a bubble is high volume levels of trade at prices that are significantly out of line with actual intrinsic values. A simpler definition is the trading of assets that have over inflated values. Bubbles are also called market bubbles, speculative bubbles, balloons, financial bubbles, and speculation mania. Prices within bubbles can vary wildly. At times, they are no longer predictable using the traditional market determining forces of only supply and demand.

There are countless explanations offered for the reasons that bubbles occur even when there is no speculation, uncertainty, or limited rationality in the market. Some have theorized that bubbles could be caused in the end by prices coordinating against each other and by changing social scenarios. Bubbles are generally identified with certainty after they have burst, in the light of drastic drops in prices. This results from the difficulty of ascertaining real intrinsic values in actual trading markets. Bubbles burst, sometimes violently, in what is known as a crash or a bursting bubble.

Mainstream economics holds that you can not predict or call bubbles before they happen or while they are forming. It argues that you can not stop bubbles from developing, and that attempting to gently prick the bubbles leads to financial crises. This school of economic thought favors authorities waiting vigilantly for bubbles to burst by themselves, so that they can handle the aftermath of the bursting bubble with fiscal and monetary policy tools.

The Austrian school of economics argues that such economic bubbles are most always negative in their impacts on economies. This is because bubbles lead to misappropriation of economic resources to inefficient and wasteful uses. The Austrian business cycle theory is based on this argument concerning bubbles.

Examples of economic bubbles abound within the U.S. economy. In the 1970's, as the United States departed from the gold standard, American monetary expansion led to enormous bubbles in commodities. Such bubbles finally ended after the Federal Reserve tightened up massively on the excess money supply by increasing the interest rates to in excess of

14%. This led to the bursting of the commodities bubble that caused gold and oil to fall down to more historically normal levels.

Another example of price bubbles proved to be the rising housing and stock market bubbles created by the extended period of low interest rates that the Federal Reserve enacted from 2001 to 2004. These bubbles burst once the interest rates returned to more normal levels.

An enormous amount of dislocation occurred in the following years as this bubble burst rippled over to the financial system and the entire economy in 2007 and 2008. The Great Recession and financial collapse were created in the wake of this bursting bubble. This example demonstrates how the larger bubbles grow before they finally pop, the more dangerous and damaging they become when they finally do burst.

Business Cycle

Business Cycle refers to changes in economic activity which economies around the globe undergo in a certain time-frame. Such cycles are generally framed under the concepts of recession or expansion. When an economy is expanding, it is growing in true terms, which means faster than inflation. This is demonstrated with economic indicators such as industrial production, personal income levels, employment levels, and consumer goods sales.

Conversely in times of economic recession, the economy is shrinking. Economists measure this with the same economic indicators as with expansion. In expansions, analysts measure the period from the bottom called the trough of the prior business cycle to the height (or peak) of the present cycle. With recessions, they instead measure them from the peak up to the trough.

There are organizations which decide what the official technical dates for any such business cycles actually are. Within the U.S., the group that makes these calls is the NBER National Bureau of Economic Research. The American NBER has decided for official purposes that fully 11 business cycles have occurred between the years of 1945 and 2009. They have also broken down the average times of such cycles.

The average business cycle length has run approximately 69 months. This means that they typically last for slightly under six years. Meanwhile, the average expansion in that time frame has run for 58.4 months long. In the same time period, the average length of contraction has amounted to a mere 11.1 months. This is good news as recessions or contractions are often painful and sometimes deep, bringing unemployment and financial hardship on millions of individuals.

The business cycle is also useful for investment positioning. Personal investors can effectively utilize it to allocate and position their various investments and funds. Looking at an example helps to clarify this idea. When an expansion is underway in the early months and years, the best cyclical stocks in different industries like technology and commodities usually outperform the other sectors. Within the recessionary periods, it is more effective to position in defensive sectors. These include consumer staples, health care, and utilities. Such segments commonly outperform their peers as they possess high and dependable dividend yields and reliable cash flows.

The NBER declared (per January of 2014) that the prior expansion began at the end of the Global Financial Crisis and Great Recession which ended officially in June of 2009. This represents the point when the Great Recession that held from years 2007 to 2009 attained its trough.

Economists consider that expansion is the normal mode of the American and Western based economies. Recessions are commonly far shorter and less frequent as well. Many people have wondered why recessions must happen. There is no general consensus among economists. Usually though, a definitive and destructive pattern of speculation that becomes carried away reveals itself in the end stages of the prior expansion. This is the case with many different business cycles.

As an example, the recession from 2001 had a mania which former Federal Reserve Chairman Alan Greenspan referred to as "Irrational Exuberance" that came before it. In this time, the various technology and especially "dot-com" stocks went from boom to bust in a short matter of months. Similarly the recession of 2007 to 2009 came after a time when real estate activity, primarily in housing, had experienced its greatest speculation in American history.

Since the 1990s began, the average time span for expansions has grown substantially. With the last three business cycles that ran from July of 1990 through June of 2009, the average expansion ran for 95 months, nearly eight years. At the same time, the typical recession lasted around 11 months. Some overly optimistic economists believed that this somehow meant the business cycles were finished.

This euphemistic hope became dashed when the world financial markets, banks, and economies melted down in spectacular free fall from 2007 to 2009. During this terrible time in the global economy, the majority of stock markets throughout the world suffered eye-watering declines exceeding even 50 percent in only 18 months. This amounted to the most severe contraction worldwide since the Great Depression of the 1930s.

Capital Appreciation

Capital appreciation refers to the increase in an asset's value. This gain is based on the increase in the market price of the asset. It primarily happens as the asset which an investor backed goes for a greater market price than the investor first paid for the asset in question. The part of the asset which is considered to be capital appreciating covers the entire market value which exceeds the cost basis, or original amount invested.

There are two principle sources of returns on investment. The largest of these is typically the capital appreciating component of the return. The other return source is from dividends or interest income. The total return of an investment results from the inclusion of both the appreciation of capital and the dividend return or interest income.

There are a wide variety of reasons why capital appreciation can occur in the first place. These differ from one asset class or market to the next, but the idea is the same. With financial assets like stocks or hard assets such as real estate, this can occur similarly.

Examples of this appreciation of capital abound. If a stock investor buys shares for $20 a piece while the stock provides a yearly dividend of $2, then the dividend yield is ten percent. A year after this, if the stock is trading at $30 and the investor obtained the $2 dividend, then the investor has enjoyed a return of $10 in capital appreciating since the stock increased from $20 to $30. The percent return of the stock price increase amounts to a capital appreciating level of 50 percent. With the $2 dividend return, the dividend yield is another ten percent. That makes the combined capital appreciation between the stock price increase and the dividend payout $12, or 60 percent. This stunning total return would please most any investor in the world.

A variety of different causes can lead to this appreciation of capital for a given asset. A generally rising trend can support the prices of the investment. These can come from such macroeconomic factors as impressive GDP growth or accommodative policies of the Federal Reserve in lowering their benchmark interest rates. It might also be something more basic having to do with the company that issued the stock itself. Stock prices could rise when the firm is outperforming the prior expectations of analysts. The real estate value of a house or other property could increase because it has good proximity to upcoming new developments like major roads, shopping centers, or good schools.

Mutual funds are another investment example which seeks out capital appreciation. The funds hunt for investments which will likely increase in value because of their undervalued but solid fundamentals or because they have earnings which outperform analysts' expectations. It is true that such investments often entail larger risks than those alternatives picked for income generation or preservation of capital, as with municipal bonds, government bonds, or high dividend paying stocks.

This is why those funds which focus on capital appreciation are deemed to be more appropriate for those investors who have a higher tolerance for risk. Growth funds are usually called capital appreciation investments since they pour their funds into company stocks which are rapidly expanding and boosting their shareholder values at the same time. They do employ capital appreciation as their primary investment strategy to meet the expectations of lifestyle and retirement investors.

Capital Gains Tax

Capital Gains Tax refers to as United States' government assessed tax on capital gains. To better understand this idea, you must first grasp what capital gains actually are. Capital gains occur as individuals sell assets at a greater price than those at which they originally purchased them, known as the cost basis. Besides capital gains, there can also be capital losses. These occur in those instances when individuals sell assets for lower prices than those at which they initially bought them.

It is critically important to realize that Capital gains taxes only accrue at a set percentage on capital gains which are actually realized. This matters hugely as such gains only become realized after the owner sells the assets. Unrealized capital gains are those which occur as the assets in question gain in value but the owners do not sell them. It is up to the Internal Revenue Service to decide the rules on these capital gains taxes. Their rules state clearly that they may only levy such taxes on any capital gains for assets which the owner has both sold and collected.

It is always helpful to look at a few clear examples to clearly understand an involved concept. For investors who buy Apple stock at $145 per share and then watch it rise to $195, they have an unrealized gain of $50 per share. By keeping the Apple stock shares, the IRS is unable to tax these considerable gains per share. Yet when investors sell said shares of stock to lock in and cash out of these $50 per share profits, they become a realized capital gain. This event makes them taxable.

The same case is true with jewelry. Individuals could purchase a diamond necklace for $20,000 one year then sell it for $22,000 the following year. This $2,000 gain becomes realized as the owner sells the necklace. The Internal Revenue Service would then get its cut.

It is critical to understand which types of assets fall under the category of eligible for Capital gains tax. In theory every personally owned item is an asset which qualifies. In practice the most usually taxable assets are financial securities and instruments, valuable collectibles (such as art, coins, and stamps), and real estate. Securities would be any type of investment with value. The best examples of this are stocks, mutual funds, options, and bonds. Dividends that investors obtain from REIT's Real Estate Investment Trusts and some mutual funds the IRS also gathers under its capital gains tax umbrella.

The same is true with real estate and real property. Any time investors or homeowners sell business or personal property and realize a profit on the transaction, this becomes a capital gain. The IRS assesses different taxable rates on business and personal properties. The sale of a primary residence enjoys substantial tax breaks from this onerous burden because of the Taxpayer Relief Act of 1997.

The law states that for any individuals who utilized a house, apartment, houseboat, or trailer as their primary residence for minimally two out of the previous five years, they are allowed to exclude as much as $500,000 of capital gains from the property sale for tax purposes. This amount applies to married couples filing jointly. Those who file as individuals only can exclude out as much as $250,000. Only profits which exceed these amounts would be taxable.

It is also important to keep in mind that the IRS prefers longer-term investments to shorter-term ones. This is why they assess higher capital gains tax rates on shorter held investments than they do on the longer ones. Every asset class also can have its own particular holding periods for what constitutes short or long term investments.

Case Shiller Index

The Case Shiller Index represents the collection of United States' Home Price Indices. These were developed by economists Karl Case and noted Yale Professor Robert Shiller. The two men's company Case Shiller Weiss, Inc. produced the statistics from 1991-2002. Allan Weiss their partner oversaw the production and release of the index on a regular basis.

This index is a collection of house price indicators for where the market has come and currently is. Among the many versions of the Case Shiller Index is the 20 city composite, the 10 city composite, and also twenty metro individual regions. The commercial versions of the Case Shiller Indices data points start in January of 1987 and run to date.

CoreLogic has since taken over the production of the index where David Stiff and Linda Ladner assumed direction. There is now a wide variety in this Case Shiller Index because Standard & Poor's 500 produces and owns a number of them. For example, Standard & Poor's publishes the Case Shiller twenty cities, condominium indices, high, medium, and low tier home price indices, and the national U.S. index. Anyone who is interested in following them can do so on the S&P company website. Eleven of the various S&P produced indices can be traded as futures on the Chicago Mercantile Exchange. Standard and Poor's set their value to a level of 100 for the prices based in January 2000.

Robert Shiller and Karl Case calculated the original Case Shiller Index on a different basis. Their index gathered home price data back to 1890. In their calculations, the 100 value was based on the house prices for the index in 1890. Robert Shiller's version of the index on his website comes out quarterly. His calculations are probably different than the ones Standard and Poor's uses as is his reference point. This is why in 2013 for the fourth quarter, the S&P 20 city index showed in the 160s, while the same point for Robert Shiller's data was in the 130s.

Professor Shiller wrote and published a book in 2000 about the housing market called Irrational Exuberance. In this book, he made the statement that no other country in the world seems to have published this type of housing data going back to the 1890s.

There are some important economic inferences that the Case Shiller Index shows. Shiller also detailed these in his book. He insists the idea that housing prices have been in a continuing uptrend over time in the United States is false. Instead, the prices of houses have a powerful tendency to go back towards their levels in 1890 as adjusted for inflation. He also notes that there is no correlation between changing home price patterns and the changes in population levels, interest rates, or even construction costs.

The Case Shiller Index also gives Shiller enough information to explain why there is no constant uptrend in the inflation adjusted home prices. Part of this is mobility. He has stated that if the prices of houses rise enough then people can simply move to another area of the country. This is because urban land makes up less than 3% of the U.S. total land area.

Improvements in technology are another reason Shiller has discussed for this phenomenon. As technology of home construction has consistently improved, it has become quicker and less expensive to build houses. This keeps a lid on the inflation adjusted cost of homes.

Between these reasons, Shiller argues that there is no trend in home prices either up or down. He has observed this not only in the United States, but also in other countries. The real house price indices of Norway and the Netherlands show the same truth.

Cash Flow Quadrant

The cash flow quadrant is a diagram that shows four types of individuals involved in a business. These four people make up the entire business world. The four quadrants are E, S, B, and I.

The E quadrant stands for employees. Employees have the same core values in general. This is security. When any employee sits down with a manager or a president, they will always tell them the same thing. This is that they are looking for a secure and safe job that includes benefits.

The S in the cash flow quadrant represents a small business owner or a self employed person. They are generally solo actors or one person outfits. These types would rather operate on their own, as their motto is always to have something done right, you should do it yourself.

On the right side of the cash flow quadrant are the B's. B stands for Big Business people. Big businesses have five hundred or greater numbers of employees. They are completely different from the others in the quadrants, as they are constantly looking for the most intelligent and capable people, networks, and systems to aid them in running their large business. They do not want to micro manage the company themselves, rather they want good people to do it on their behalf.

The last quarter of the cash flow quadrants is the I, which stands for Investor. Investors are those individuals who make money work effectively and efficiently for themselves. The main difference between them and the B quadrants it that the investors have their money working hard while the Big Business people have other people working hard for them. Both groups of B's and I's represent the wealthy. The employees and the self employed are the people who work hard for the business people and investors on the right, or wealthy side of the quadrant.

The cash flow quadrant explains the differences between the rich and the working poor. It is useful to describe four types of income that a person can generate as well. The smartest people in the cash flow quadrant are the ones who manage to make the other people and their money work hard for their benefit. That is why they are the wealthy, while the hard working members of society on the left side are the ones who do all of the working on the wealthy people's behalf. Learning to become wealthy means effectively changing which square of the cash flow quadrant a person occupies.

Certificate of Title

A certificate of title represents a document which states who the owners or owner of real estate or personal property actually are. It is issued by a municipal or state government. This certificate gives evidence of any ownership rights.

In general a title insurance company will issue a certificate of title opinion on a house or piece of property. This is their statement of opinion regarding the status of a title. They draft this opinion after carefully looking through public records pertaining to the property.

Such a certificate of title opinion will not necessarily assure the buyer of a clean title. It will list out any encumbrance on the property. Encumbrances are often items that keep the property from being freely sold. These could include easements or liens. The title companies will issue such certificates to financial institutions which are making the loan. Many of these lenders must have such documents in hand before they will approve a mortgage loan for a house or piece of property.

Certificates of title are extremely important with real estate. This is why a title company will issue their opinion that the person selling the property actually owns it. Personal property is easier to give to another person than is land. Where land is concerned, a person might be living on a given property and yet not own it. This makes the certificate opinion from the title company critical. It promises that the company has performed the complete background check regarding who owns the land and so has the right to sell it.

This certificate of title is a statement of fact when a state or municipal government actually issues it. These documents contain a good deal of useful information on them. All of them will have the name and address of the owner of the property. They also have information that identifies the property itself in some specific way.

If the certificate pertains to a real estate property, then it will have the location of or address for the land in question. If it is instead for a car or other vehicle, it will have the license plate number and possibly the vehicle identification number. These certificates will also state what the encumbrance is on the property if there is any. If there is a lien on a vehicle or mortgage on the house or land, this will be noted.

State agencies will also issue certificates of title on a variety of vehicles. This covers such things as buses, trucks, motorcycles, trailers, motor homes, boats and watercraft, and airplanes. When a lender makes a loan on such a vehicle, it is able to keep the title in its possession until the debt has been paid in full. They then release the lien at this point and send back the title certificate to the actual owner.

Certificates of title should not be confused with deeds though they share certain common characteristics. Each of these two documents offers a proof of ownership for the property in question. The certificate of title has sufficient information to specifically identify the property itself and any relevant encumbrances. Deeds have additional information on the real property. This includes any conditions for the ownership as well as more detailed information on and about the property. Deeds are critical elements in any transfer of real estate.

Cession Deed

A cession deed is used to give up property rights to a government authority. It is possible for individuals, companies, or organizations to sign a cession deed with a state or the federal government in the U.S. Cession deeds have generally been utilized between great imperial powers like the United States or Great Britain and smaller independent entities such as islands or Indian tribes ruled by chieftains. Both American Samoa and the British colony of Fiji were created by a cession deed in the 1800's.

American Samoa arose because of the Deed of Cession of Tutuila. The local chiefs from the island of Tutuila signed this treaty with the United States on April 17, 1900. As part of the cession deed, the chiefs ceded their island to the U.S. and swore allegiance to the country. Four years later in 1904, the chiefs of neighboring island Manu'a also agreed to cede their territory to the U.S.

In exchange for this, the chiefs received guarantees that they could continue to exercise control over their individual villages. Their rule had to be maintained according to the American laws that pertained to Samoa. The control also could not obstruct any advances of civilization or the peace of the people over which they ruled. The U.S. promised to protect and respect the rights of the inhabitants, particularly their property and land rights.

Congress did not ratify this cession deed until the Ratification Act of 1929. The navy administered this new American Samoa during the years of 1900 to 1951. At that point the President of the U.S. issued executive order 10264 and transferred control of the American Samoa territory to the Secretary of the Interior. American Samoa has been a territory of the U.S. with a locally elected governor, lieutenant governor, and legislative assembly since the 1960s. The territory is self governing under its constitution that took effect in 1967.

The British Empire also signed a cession deed when in gained control of the Kingdom of Fiji. This process began in 1871 when the British honorary consul John Bates Thurston persuaded the other chiefs of Fiji to accept the great war chieftain Cakobau as constitutional monarch. Actual power resided in the legislature and cabinet that the Australian cotton settlers dominated. The assembly had its first meeting in November 1871 in Levuka.

This constitutional monarchy arrangement did not work out well for Fiji. The government spent more money than it had and built up an unmanageable debt in only a matter of months. Two years of economic and social unrest followed in the islands kingdom. At this point, Cakobau asked the British consul Thurston to talk with the British government about ceding control of the islands to the empire. This was the second time Cakobau had attempted to cede his control to Great Britain.

Two British commissioners came to Fiji to consider the practicalities of annexing Fiji. Cakobau presented a final offer on March 21, 1874. The British accepted this deal. Sir Hercules Robinson who was eventually to be appointed governor arrived in September on British naval ship Dido. Cakobau enjoyed a royal 21 gun salute as Robinson received him.

King Cakobau, rival chief Ma'afu, and other senior Fijian Chiefs signed two separate copies of the Deed of Cession on October 10, 1874. One copy remained in Fiji while the other copy went back to Great Britain. The British ruled Fiji for the next ninety-six years under a series of appointed governors before granting the island nation its independence.

Chain of Title

A chain of title refers to the consecutive historical transfers in a title on a particular piece of real estate property. These chains start with the current owner of the property and trace their way back to the property's first owner. Reconstructing such a chain can be extremely important when a lender needs complete ownership documentation. Such title documents are generally kept by registry offices with local and municipal governments.

The field of real estate places tremendous importance on such a chain of title. Because it can be difficult to construct them, companies have come up with systems to track ownership and registration of real estate property. One of these is the Torrens Title system.

Insurance companies in the United States will provide title insurance on a property. They do this using the chain of title on real estate that the owners are transferring. These chains are so important that many title insurance companies will keep their own private title operations to track such titles so they do not have to rely on only official government records. In cases where it is difficult to come up with a complete chain, abstracts of title can be utilized. Attorneys will sometimes certify these.

Lack of a clear chain of title has caused significant problems during the Great Recession of 2008. These problems began when many lending companies made the choice in 1995 to use an electronic registry to hold the title. The best known company in this arena was MERS Mortgage Electronic Registration Systems. The banks tried to use this system so they could sell and purchase mortgages without needing to register ownership changes with the appropriate local governments. Without clear title chains, the banks were often not able to come up with the original titles needed to force foreclosures and evictions as individuals defaulted on their mortgages. A number of states throughout the U.S. sued the banks over these actions.

The chain of title is also utilized in intellectual property areas. With the film industry, they refer to documentation that demonstrates the ownership rights of a particular movie. These chains can be used in other creative endeavors in the movie business. If many individuals contributed to the creative work, authorship is owned by a large number of the writers. Film distributors and buyers must carefully examine these chains of title to know the proprietary rights or rights under license of the owner. This is also important with books and encyclopedias.

Documents on chains of title for films can include a number of other intellectual properties. Trademarks can be included. Musical copyrights often form part of these chains as well. Talent agreements are an important part of these. They provide the talent's legal release to utilize their images, works, appearance, and personal rights in movies. This covers everyone from directors to actors to choreographers and cinematographers. There are even insurance policies that cover omissions and errors of movie producers who do not obtain sufficient chains of title.

Specific organizations compile these reports for copyright property on behalf of the movie studios. To do so, they consult with the U.S. Copyright Office regarding author claimants, screening searches, and registration renewal searches. This detailed work requires that records from the Copyright Office dating back to 1870 and extending to the present be consulted. There are also other databases and trade publications which have to be reviewed for possible ownership claims.

Chapter 11 Bankruptcy

Chapter 11 Bankruptcy proves to be a specific type of bankruptcy. This kind has to do with the business assets, debts, and affairs being reorganized. The business reorganization filing was named for the Section 11 of the United States' Bankruptcy Code. Corporations commonly file it that need some time to rearrange the terms of their debts and their business operations. It gives them a fresh start on repaying their debt obligations. Naturally the indebted company will have to stick to the terms of the reorganization plan. This proves to be the most highly complex type of bankruptcy filing possible. Companies have been advised to only entertain it once they have contemplated their other options and analyzed the repercussions of such a filing.

This Chapter 11 bankruptcy rarely makes the news unless it is a nationally known or famous corporation which is filing. Among the major corporations that have filed such a Chapter 11 bankruptcy are United Airlines, General Motors, K-Mart, and Lehman Brothers. The first three successfully emerged from it and became as great or stronger than they were before falling into hard times financially. In reality, the vast majority of these cases are unknown to the general public. As an example, in the year 2010, nearly 14,000 separate corporations filed for Chapter 11.

The point of this Chapter 11 Bankruptcy is to assist a corporation in restructuring both obligations and debts. The goal is not to close down the business. In fact it rarely leads to the corporation closing. Instead, corporations like K-mart, General Motors, and tens of thousands of others were able to survive and once again thrive thanks to the useful process of protection from creditors and reorganization of business debts.

It is typically LLCs Limited Liability Companies, partnerships, and corporations that make application for Chapter 11 Bankruptcy. There are cases where individuals who are positively saddled with debt and who are not able to be approved for a Chapter 13 or Chapter 7 filing can be qualified for Chapter 11 instead. The time table for successfully completing Chapter 11 bankruptcy ranges from several months to as long as two years.

Businesses that are in the middle of their Chapter 11 cases are encouraged to keep operating. The debtor in possession will typically run the business normally. Where there are cases that have gross incompetence, dishonest dealings, or even fraud involved, typically trustees come in to take over the business and its daily operations while the bankruptcy proceedings are ongoing.

Corporations in the midst of these filings will not be permitted to engage in specific decisions without first having to consult with the courts to proceed. They may not terminate or sign rental agreements, sell any assets beyond regular inventory, or expand existing business operations or alternatively cease them. The bankruptcy court retains full control regarding any hiring and paying of lawyers as well as signing contracts with either unions or vendors. Lastly, such indebted organizations and entities may not sign for a loan that will pay once the bankruptcy process finishes.

After the business or person files their chapter 11 bankruptcy, it gains the right to offer a first reorganization plan. Such plans often include renegotiating owed debts and reducing the company size in order to slash expenses. There are some scenarios where the plan will require every asset to be liquidated in order to pay off the creditors, as with Lehman Brothers.

When plans are fair and workable, courts will approve them. This moves the reorganization process ahead. For plans to be accepted, they also have to maintain the creditors' best interests for the future repayment of debts owed to them. When the debtor can not or will not put forward a plan of their own for reorganization, then the creditors are invited to offer one in the indebted company or person's place.

Chapter 7 Bankruptcy

Chapter 7 bankruptcy is a form of protection from creditors. Unlike Chapter 13 bankruptcy, it does not have any repayment plan. In the Chapter 7 a bankruptcy trustee determines what eligible assets the debtor individual or company has. The trustee then collects these available assets, sells them, and distributes proceeds to the creditors against their debts. This is all done under the rules of the Bankruptcy Code.

Debtors are permitted to keep specific property that is exempt, such as their house. Other property that the debtor holds will be mortgaged or have liens put against it to pledge it to the various creditors until it is liquidated. Debtors who file chapter 7 will likely forfeit property in partial payment of debts.

Chapter 7 bankruptcy is available to corporations, partnerships, and individuals who pass a means test. The relief can be granted whether or not the debtor is ruled to be insolvent.

Chapter 7 bankruptcy cases start when debtors file their petitions with their particular area's bankruptcy court. For businesses, they use the address where the main office is located. Debtors are required to give the court information that includes schedules of current expenditures and income and liabilities and assets.

They are also required to furnish a financial affairs statement and a schedule of contracts and leases which are not expired. The debtors will also have to deliver the trustee tax return copies from the most current tax year along with any tax returns which they file while the case is ongoing.

Debtors who are individuals also have to furnish their court with other documents. They are required to file a credit counseling certificate and any repayment plan created there. They must also file proof of income from employers 60 days before their original filing, a monthly income statement along with expected increases in either, and notice of interest they have in tuition or state education accounts. Husbands and wives are allowed to file individually or jointly. They must abide by the requirements for individual debtors either way.

The courts are required to charge debtors who file $335 in filing, administrative, and trustee fees. Debtors typically pay these when they file to the clerk of court. The court can give permission for individuals to pay by installments instead. When the income of debtor's proves to be less than 150% of the amount of the poverty level, the court can choose to drop the fee requirements.

Debtors will have to provide a great amount of information in order to complete their Chapter 7 filing and receive a discharge of debts. They have to list out each of their creditors along with the amounts they owe then and the type of claim. Debtors have to furnish a list of all property the own. They must also give the information on the amount, source, and frequency of income they have to the court.

Finally, they will be required to provide an in depth list of all monthly living expenses that includes housing, utilities, food, transportation, clothing, medicine, and taxes. This helps the court to determine if the debtor is able to set up a repayment plan instead of discharging the debts.

From 21 to 40 days after the debtor files the petition with the courts, the trustee hosts a creditors' meeting. The debtor will have to cooperate with the trustee on any requests for additional financial documents or records. At this meeting, the trustee will ask questions to make sure the debtor is fully aware of the consequences of debt discharge by the bankruptcy court. Sometimes trustees will deliver this in written form to the debtor before or at the meeting. Assuming the trustee makes the recommendation for discharge, the Federal bankruptcy court judge will discharge the debts when the process is completed.

Closing Costs

Closing costs are the fees that are charged when you buy a house. Many other costs are associated with buying a house than only the down payment. These closing costs are fees like recording fees, title policies, courier charges, inspections, lender fees, and start up reserve fees to create an impound account.

The most expensive component of these closing costs is the lender charged fees. Such closing costs are charged beyond the home's purchase price. Most closing costs are set and predetermined, meaning that they are not open to negotiation.

The total price of closing costs is fairly standard. Typically, a good guideline for closing costs is that they will run you somewhere between two and four percent of a house's purchase price. The range is as large as this spread because the origination fees and points for making the loan vary significantly from one lender to the next. These points and origination fees that are charged by the lender are always revealed to a buyer in the Good Faith Estimates that are provided to the buyers. For example, a home that is $400,000 will have closing costs that run from around $4,000 to $16,000. They could be even higher than this amount, on some occasions.

Some closing costs are of the non-recurring kind. Such fees are charged to a buyer of a house on only a single time. They include escrow or closing, title policies, courier fees, wire fees, notary charges, endorsements, attorney costs, city or county or state transfer taxes, recording, natural hazard disclosures, home protection plans, lender fees for the HUD-1 800 line, and home inspections.

Other closing costs are called prepaid closing costs, or recurring closing costs. Although these are paid for in a single lump sump up front, they cover those costs that continue to recur throughout the life of the home loan. There are comprised of property taxes, flood insurance when required, fire insurance premiums, prepaid interest, and private or mutual mortgage insurance premiums.

Closing costs are also impacted by the month of the year in which you close on the house in question. This is because future insurance and tax payments will be collected on a pro rated basis for the number of months of premiums for the year. Not all loans come with an escrow or impound account either. Yet loans that are for in excess of eighty percent of the purchase price of your house will mandate such an escrow account and impound be established.

Closing costs are some of the unfortunately high expenses associated with buying a house. They are only avoidable when a person takes over an assumable mortgage. In these cases, most closing costs, such as lender points and origination fees, are side stepped by a buyer.

Collateral

Collateral refers to an asset or piece of Real Estate which borrowers provide as security to lenders in exchange for a loan. This property actually secures the mortgage or other form of loan. In the event that the borrowers do not continue to make the agreed upon payments on the loan according to the laid out schedule, the financial institution has the right to seize this property in order to recover the principal losses.

Because such collateral provides at least nominal security to the lending institution in the scenarios where the borrower refuses to or is unable repay the loan, these forms of loans are commonly provided with lower interest rates as compared to those loans which are unsecured entirely. When such a lender has interest in the underlying property provided by the borrower then this is referred to as a lien.

In the end there are several arrangements with such collateral. The type of loan often determines which form will be required within the contract. With car loans or mortgages, the loans are secured by the property upon which the financial institution issues the loan. Other forms of loans have more flexible security, as with collateralized personal loans. In order for any loan to be called secured, the backing security has to be at least equal to or greater than the balance that remains on the loan in question.

Such secured loans entail far less risk for lenders because the underlying property serves as an incentive for the borrower to keep paying back the loan. Borrowers know all too well that if they do not complete the required payments then the financial institution which holds the loan may legally possess (or repossess) this collateral in order to recoup the money it is owed on the rest of the loan.

With mortgages, the collateral in question will always be the home that the borrower buys using the loan in the first place. If and when they fail to pay the debts, then the lender may seize possession of the property by utilizing a procedure called foreclosure. After the lender completes the necessary court process and has the property back in its possession, it is allowed to sell off the home to someone else. This will permit the bank to cover the principal which remains on the original loan along with their costs for the foreclosure.

Houses also can also be utilized for second mortgage collateral, or against HELOC's (Home Equity Lines of Credit). In such scenarios, the credit delivered by the financial institution may not be greater than the equity which exists within the home itself. As a tangible example, a home could have a market value of $300,000. At the same time, it might be that $175,000 of the original mortgage balance remains to pay. This would mean that the majority of HELOC's or even second mortgages would not exceed the available equity of $125,000.

Collateral is also utilized in margin accounts' trading of stocks, commodities, and futures. In this case, it is the securities themselves that become the property which secures the brokerage loan. In the event that a margin call has to be issued and the account holder will not or can not pay it on demand, then the securities' value ultimately makes certain that the brokerage will get back its loaned money.

Sometimes financial institutions will require additional collateral be put up for a given existing loan, if the contract allows such a scenario. This will reduce increasing risks for the lending institution. A creditor could give notice that without such additional security, they will be forced to raise the interest rate on the loan. Additionally accepted security could be certificates of deposit, cash, equipment, letters of credit, or even shares of stock.

Collateralized Mortgage Obligation (CMO)

Collateralized mortgage obligations are investments that contain home mortgages. These mortgages underlie the securities themselves. These CMO yields and results derive from the home mortgage loans' performance on which they are based. This is true with other mortgage backed securities as well.

Lenders sell these loans to an intermediary firm. Such an intermediary pools these loans together and issues certificates based on them. Investors are able to buy these certificates to earn the principal and interest payments from the mortgages. The payments these homeowners make go through the intermediary firm before finally reaching the investors who bought them.

The performance of collateralized mortgage obligations depends on the track record of the mortgage payers. What makes them different from other types of mortgage backed securities is that it is not only a single loan on which they are based. Rather they are categorized by groups of loans according to the payment period for the mortgages within the pool itself.

Issuers set up CMOs this way to try to reduce the effects of a mortgage being prepaid. This can often be a problem for investments based on only a single mortgage as owners refinance their loans and pay off the initial one on which the investment was based. With the CMOs, the risk of home owners defaulting is spread across a number of different mortgages and shared by many investors.

Tranches are the different categories within the mortgage pools on which the collateralized mortgage obligations are based. The tranches are often divided according to the mortgage repayment schedules of the loans. For each tranche, the issuer creates bonds with different interest rates and maturity dates. These CMO bonds can come with maturity dates of twenty, ten, five, and two years. The bondholders of each individual tranche receive the coupon or interest payments out of the mortgage pool. Principal payments accrue initially to those bonds in the first tranche which mature soonest.

The bonds on collateralized mortgage obligations turn out to be highly rated. This is especially the case when they are backed by GSE government mortgages and similar types of high grade loans. This means that the risk of default is low compared with other mortgage backed securities.

There are three types of groups who issue these CMOs. The FHLMC Federal Home Loan Mortgage Corporation issues many of them. Other GSE Government Sponsored Enterprises like Ginnie Mae provide them as well. There are also private companies which issue these CMOs. Many investors consider the ones issued by the government agencies to be less risky, but this is not necessarily the case. The government is not required to bail out the GSEs and their CMOs.

There are investors who choose to hold their CMO bonds until they mature. Others will re-sell or buy them using the secondary market. The prices for these investments on this market go up and down based on any changes in the interest rates.

The other most common type of mortgage backed securities besides these CMOs are pass through securities. Pass throughs are usually based on a single or few mortgages set up like a trust that collects and passes through the interest and principal repayments.

Common Securitization Platform (CSP)

During the financial crisis that started back in 2008, the federal government took control of both Fannie Mae and Freddie Mac the government sponsored enterprises because they became insolvent. One of the ideas that the since-then managing agency the FHFA Federal Housing Finance Agency came up with is the Common Securitization Platform. This strategic goal resulted from the FHFAs *2014 Strategic Plan for the Conservatorships of Fannie Mae and Freddie Mac* report.

The hope with this Common Securitization Platform is to create a new and greatly improved securitization infrastructure for both Freddie Mac and Fannie Mae. These two groups are collectively known as the Enterprises. Their new platform is to be for American mortgage loans which are backed up by single family kinds of properties.

In order to put this vision into reality, the two GSEs have established a joint venture called CSS Common Securitization Solutions. It is actually designing the Common Securitization Platform under the leadership and direction of the FHFA. The CSS fills the role of agent for both enterprises to help with issuing the single family mortgage securities. It also is handling disclosures when the securities are issued and in the future. Besides this, CSS is administering such securities after they are issued.

Among the more important tasks the Common Securitization Solutions is carrying out with regards to the program surrounds the operational capabilities of the Common Securitization Platform. CSS is responsible for creating these so that the CSP will run. The CSP will eventually support the securitizing activities of the GSEs and their single family mortgage program. This will culminate in the two Enterprises issuing one Single Security, which will actually be a single mortgage backed security.

Issuing this Single Security is important for several reasons. The FHFA along with Fannie Mae and Freddie Mac all want to see their securities' all around liquidity improve. This will also aid in the mission of the two GSEs to ensure the country's housing finance markets remain liquid too.

Common Securitization Platform is both a technology and operating platform then. In the future, it will handle a great number of the critical back office functions and operations of the Single Security. It will also take over the majority of the two GSEs present securitization operations in the single family mortgages for them. Without the CSP, it would be practically impossible to actually launch and integrate the Single Security.

Single Security is the future of Freddie Mac and Fannie Mae. It will help to ensure that adequate financing for fixed rate mortgages and loans continues for the one unit to four unit single family properties. The way that it will actually do this is by taking elements from both of the GSEs and combining the best of each.

There are three areas where these different procedures have to be aligned for the Single Security to function properly. The key features of the Fannie Mae mortgage backed securities and the Freddie Mac participation certificates will be taken mostly from Fannie's mortgage backed securities model. Investor disclosures will be modeled after Freddie's participation certificates. A final area to be aligned concerns the practices and policies that will be utilized to take loans out of securities.

The Single Security endeavor also promises to allow for some exchanges of old for new securities. This pertains particularly to the 45 day Participation Certificates of Freddie Mac. These will be exchangeable for 55 day time frame Single Securities that Freddie Mac will issue.

Compound Interest

Compound interest represents interest which calculates on both the original principal amount as well as the interest that was accumulated previously during the loan or investment. Economists have called this miraculous phenomenon an interest on interest. It causes loans or invested deposits to increase at a significantly faster pace than only simple interest, the opposite of compound interest. Simple interest proves to be interest that calculates on just the principal amount of money.

Compound interest accrues at an interest rate which determines how often the compounding occurs. The higher the compound interest rate turns out to be, the faster the principal will compound and the more compounding periods will occur. Consider an example of how effective compounding truly is. $100 that is compounded at a rate of 10% per year will turn out to be less than $100 which is compounded at only 5% but semi annually during the same length of time.

Compound interest is important to individuals as it is able to take a few dollars worth of savings now and transform them into significant money throughout lifetimes. Investors do not need an MBA or a Wall Street background in order to benefit from this principle. Practically all investments earn compounding interest if the owners leave these earnings in the investment account over the long term.

This form of interest cuts both ways on the receiving and paying sides. When individuals are saving and investing money, it helps them grow the amount faster. When they are borrowing and paying the same interest on the debt, it grows against them faster. Individuals who are saving wish their money to compound as often as they can. Individuals who are borrowing wish it to compound as infrequently as possible. Savers are better off if they are able to compound quarterly instead of annually while just the opposite is true for borrowers.

For people who are compounding their investments, time works on their side. Money that grows at a rate of 6% each year doubles every 12 years. This means that it increases to four times as much as the original amount in only 24 years. For individuals paying compound interest, time is similarly working against them. Credit card companies utilize this principle to keep their card owners in debt forever by encouraging them to only make minimum monthly payments on the bills.

Thanks to compounding, a smaller amount of money that a person adds to an account upfront is more valuable than a larger sum of money he or she adds decades later. This cuts both ways. By paying down principal on a credit card with an extra $5 per month, the amount of compound interest individuals pay on a 14% interest rate credit card decreases by $1,315 over ten years. This is true even though they have paid only $600 in extra payments over this amount of time.

Anyone can make the miracle of compounding work for them. The idea works the same whether individuals are investing $100 or $100 million instead. Millionaires have greater ranges of investment choices. Even relatively poor people can compound their interest to increase their original amount and double their money as often as possible.

Compounding interest means that participants have to give up using some dollars today in order to obtain a greater benefit from them in the future. The little money may be missed now, but the rewards for the more significant amounts in the future will more than make up for the little sacrifice the individual makes now. Financial planners have claimed that the difference between poverty and financial comfort in the future amounts to even a few dollars in savings each week invested now rather than later.

Constructive Eviction

Constructive eviction is a backdoor way of evicting a tenant. It is not done through legal means because of a tenant failing to pay rent or seriously breaking the property rules. It is instead the process of a landlord making a rental uninhabitable for the tenant. Though the term sounds positive, it is quite the opposite. Landlords who engage in this type of eviction are failing to carry out their legal obligations.

For constructive eviction to take place, a residential rental property must deteriorate into enough disrepair that it becomes very difficult or near impossible to live in the property. It could also be that the landlord allows a condition to exist that makes inhabiting the home or apartment intolerable. As the condition becomes so severe that the property is no longer fit to live in, the tenant is forced to leave. An uninhabitable property exists in a state that compels the renter to move away, or to be constructively evicted. Because the renter is incapable of completely utilizing and possessing the property, he or she has been evicted technically.

There are a number of way in which a tenant could be a victim of constructive eviction. The landlord might turn off the electricity, gas, or water utilities. The owner might disregard an environmental problem such as toxic mold or flaking off lead paint and not properly clean it. He or she could also not fix leaking roofs. This causes water damage to walls and eventually leads to mold. The owners could block the unit entrance or change the locks. They might do something extreme such as take out sinks or toilets from the property as well. When the conditions deteriorate to the point that tenants abandon the rental then constructive eviction has occurred.

A landlord might engage in this type of unethical behavior because of rental controls. Many cities limit the amount by which rent can be increased. They may also allow the tenant to remain in the rental with an automatically renewing lease so long as they fulfill the contract obligations.

Tenants have the ability to fight back against this type of eviction. This starts with providing the owner a notice in writing of the constructive eviction. The landlord must be given a fair amount of time to address the issue. This may not translate to an instant repair that happens in 24 hours. Many repairs require more time to have completed. Water and gas leaks are examples of these. Still the repairs have to be done in a time frame that is reasonable.

Renters who find themselves in living conditions that are poor should take pictures. They also should invite independent inspectors to examine the property. These types of inspectors come from the permit or building department, as well as from the area health department.

When landlords are unwilling to address the uninhabitable living conditions in a reasonable time frame after having been given fair written notice, renters have rights. They are usually allowed to leave the property without having to pay rent that would still be owed according to the rental or lease agreement. In general, tenants have to move away from the property while they begin the legal process of terminating the lease and suing the owner for damages.

It is often better to compel the owner to make the necessary repairs or to address the issues that are creating the uninhabitable living conditions on the property in the first place. This is easier in cities and states that have strong legal enforcement of the landlord obligations. New York City and state are an example of places in the United States that make it difficult for owners to practice constructive eviction by requiring that they fulfill their maintenance duties.

Core Inflation

Core Inflation refers to the change in the cost of goods and services without calculating the important categories of food and energy. The U.S. federal government believes this to be the most accurate means of figuring up true inflationary trends. They claim that both energy products and food components are priced too volatilely to be a part of the core inflation calculation and figure. This is because they constantly change so rapidly that they interfere with inflation readings.

The reason for this is that they are subject to the whims of the traders on the various commodity market exchanges. The majority of core food products like beef, pork, wheat, orange juice, and more and energy products such as oil, natural gas, and gasoline trade each and every week day all throughout the day.

As an example, traders of commodities will likely bid up the prices of oil and its derivative products when they believe its supplies will diminish or if they feel that demand will outpace supplies. It could be that a strike will interrupt production and oil supplies from Nigeria, Venezuela, or Angola. Because of this fear, traders will purchase oil at the prices today and hope to sell it for a higher amount at the anticipated greater prices tomorrow or next week.

That is all that it really takes to radically increase the price of oil. Should the strike wrap up quickly, then the oil prices will plunge when traders suddenly all sell out of their positions. This is why both energy and food prices depend on rapidly changing human emotions rather than real changes to underlying forces of supply and demand. Between this and the inelastic demand of food and energy which people simply have to possess in order to live, these commodities rise and fall crazily sometimes.

Consider how gasoline prices will change when their primary input oil does. Yet as people require gas to travel to school and work, they cannot delay their purchases and wait for prices to decline. Food prices also vary according to gasoline and oil prices as they are shipped by truck throughout the United States. In truth, most foods on your dinner plate have more frequent flyer miles than you ever dreamed of acquiring.

The Fed has a few tools to deal with higher than desired core inflation. The problem comes with their tools needing time to take effect on the broader economy. This might mean as much as from six to 18 months before changes to the Fed Funds rate will show a meaningful impact on the inflation rate in the U.S. As the Fed Funds rate goes higher, so will the bank loans and mortgage rates. Credit will tighten and slow economic growth. Corporations find themselves lowering their core prices in order to keep selling merchandise. This lowers inflation as it finally all feeds through to the economy.

The Federal Reserve targets inflation with their policies. They promise to not take action when the core inflation rate remains at two percent or lower. Consider a real world example. Inflation has a tendency to creep higher throughout the summer as people go on vacations. The Fed does not wish to raise rates each summer though, which would force them to proportionally lower them again in the fall.

Rather, they wait and see if such summer increases boost the prices of the goods and services ex food and energy permanently. Yet ultimately higher food and gas prices force up the prices of all other goods and services if they remain elevated for long. This is why the Federal Reserve will also consider the headline inflation rate, which is the opposite of the core inflation rate. This broader measure of inflation considers food and energy prices alongside all other goods and services.

The core inflation rate can be measured via the Core Price Index, or core CPI, as well as the core Personal Consumption Expenditures price index, or core PCE price index.

Counter Offer

Counter offers are those made by home sellers after buyers have turned in an official offer to buy the house. Usually, such counter offers spell out the terms with which the seller will accept the buyer's official initial offer. Many different specifics can be addressed with a counter offer.

Some of these things include the consideration of a higher offering price, presenting a larger earnest money deposit, and modifying time frames for contingencies. Others counter offer elements might revolve around altering service providers, excluding any personal property from the home selling contract, or changing the possession date or closing date. A seller might also refuse to cover the costs of certain fees or reports.

Not only can sellers counter a buyer's original offer, but buyers can similarly submit counter offers back to the seller on their counter offer. This is labeled a counter-counter offer. No limit to the actual numbers of counter offers which can be handed back and forth exists.

Counter offers are easily rejected. A number of purchase contracts for houses have places at the bottom of the contract for a seller to put his or her initials if the offer is being rejected. Many offers have time frames, or expiration dates, when the offer will be rejected if the seller has not responded. Sellers can simply write the word rejected over a contract's face, then date and initial it to reject a counter offer.

In some states, sellers are allowed to come back with various counter offers at once. For example, in California, sellers are allowed to counter more than one offer at a time and every counter offer is permitted to be different. Should one of these buyers choose to affirm the counter offer of the seller in this scenario, the seller is not required to agree to the acceptance of the buyer. This can become confusing, so talking with real estate attorneys can be a good idea in these complicated cases.

Counter offers can similarly be accepted without difficulty by the buyer. All that a buyer needs to do to take the counter is to accept the offer and send it back to the entity to which it goes. Like with anything, timing is critical. Counter offers expire much as purchase offers do. This means that a seller could always elect to take an alternative offer while a buyer contemplates whether or not to sign off on the counter offer.

Even though many agents become discouraged at the mention of a counter offer being on the table, this should not be the case. Houses can be secured with new offers submitted even while a counter offer is out. In such a scenario, sellers commonly go ahead and take the second buyer offer. They then withdraw their counter offer from the first buyer. This is permissible and proper in every state.

Creditor

Creditors are those financial institutions or individuals who extend credit to a business or other individual. They carry this out by providing financing which they expect will be paid back at a set time in the future. There is another type of creditor as well. This is a company which delivers services or supplies to a person or other business yet does not insist on immediate payment. Since the customer actually does owe the company money for the goods or services provided in advance of payment, that company becomes their creditor de facto.

Within the universe of a creditor there are real and personal categories of them. Finance companies and banks represent real creditor situations. This is because they possess official and legally binding contracts which they sign with the borrower. In this action, they bind assets of the borrower as collateral against the loan in many cases. Typical collateral would be the underlying asset for which the borrower is obtaining credit in the first place. This is often a car, a house, or some other piece of Real Estate. A personal creditor is a family member of friend choosing to loan out money to their loved one or friend.

Real creditors do not loan out money out of the goodness of their hearts. Instead, they intend to earn profits by charging the borrowers interest for these loans. Looking at an example helps to clarify the concept. A creditor might loan out $10,000 to a borrower at a six percent rate of interest. The lending institution will realize earnings in the form of loan interest.

For this accommodation, the creditor is taking on some amount of risk that the borrowing business or individual might potentially default on the loan. This is why the majority of those extending credit will price the interest rate which they charge the borrower based on the business or persons' prior credit history and creditworthiness. It becomes important to borrowers of especially large amounts of money to have high credit quality so that they are able to obtain a more advantageous interest rate and save money on the interest payments.

The rates of interest on mortgages depend heavily on a host of different variables. Some of these are the nature of the lender, the credit history of the borrower, and the amount of the upfront down payment. Still, it is usually the creditworthiness that overwhelmingly determines the final interest rate which becomes applied to a loan such as a mortgage. This is because those borrowers who boast fantastic credit histories and scores come across as low risk for the creditor in question. It is why they enjoy the lowest of interest rates. As lower credit score-carrying borrowers prove to be considerably riskier for the creditors, they manage their risk by requiring a greater rate of interest in compensation.

There are cases where a creditor will not obtain repayment. In such cases, they do have several options. Banks and official real credit issuing entities are allowed to repossess the underlying collateral. This would mean they have the ability to seize either the car or home which secured the loan. Where unsecured debts are concerned, it is more difficult to collect. They might sue the borrower for the unpaid debts in these cases. Courts could choose to issue orders attempting to force the borrower to pay them back. They might do this by seizing assets in their bank accounts or by garnishing their wages with their employers.

Sometimes the borrowers will choose to file for bankruptcy. In these cases, the courts will be the ones to alert the creditor to the situation. There are cases where any non- necessary assets can be liquidated so that debts can be paid back. The order of priority will make unsecured creditors last in the receiving line.

Debt Deflation

Debt Deflation refers to the scenario where the loan collateral (or any other type of debt) sees a decrease in value. This is generally a negative end result. It often causes the loan issuer to insist on a restructure of the loan agreement. In other cases, they may be able to demand that the loan itself be completely restructured. Other phrases that describe this concept are collateral deflation and worst deflation.

Mortgages are a great example of this to consider. They are a traditional type of secured debt. If an individual takes out a mortgage to buy a house with, then the house itself proves to be the securing underlying collateral on this mortgage loan. This means that if the buyer later subsequently defaults on the payments which he or she make to the bank each month, then the bank would begin the tedious process to repossesses the house. A problem arises when the value of the house diminishes in value at the same time that the buyer is still caught up in the process of making the payments owed to the bank. This would create a potentially devastating debt deflation downward spiral and uncomfortable situation. In severe cases, this can be enough to cause a home owner to completely despair and simply walk away from the house and its associated mortgage come what may.

This actually happened back in the Subprime Mortgage Meltdown, Great Recession, and Global Financial Crisis of 2007-2009. So many homes had been purchased in the boom period of the early 2000's that when prices began to plunge on a breath taking national and regional scale, many buyers found themselves severely underwater on their mortgage loan collateral. The houses in many cases became worth significantly less than the principal balance on the loan which purchased them. Defaults went through the proverbial roof as many buyers realized that they had no realistic hope of seeing the value of the house rise back up.

It helps to look at an example of the despair this subprime mortgage crisis meltdown caused countless Americans, many of whom had been irresponsible, it is true. If a person had purchased a $300,000 priced house with a mortgage for $270,000 before 2006 peak pricing in the national housing market, then he or she might have sat helplessly by as the value of this same house subsequently plummeted by even 25 percent. It would meant that the $300,000 dream home was then only worth $225,000. Now in order for the house to again be worth just what the buyer owed on it, it would have to rise back up to the $270,000 mortgage total balance amount. This meant that the value had to increase by $45,000, or a staggering 20 percent, just to get back to even on the mortgage balance amount owed. In order for the house to be worth the actual $300,000 the buyer had originally paid out, it would have to rise by an even steeper $75,000, representing a whopping 33.3 percent. This would take years once the market actually bottomed out, itself a hopeless-looking procedure that require literally years before rock bottom was finally hit.

Nationally, home values that began to crash and burn in 2007 did not start to slowly crawl back up until 2011 to 2012, four to five long years later. A decade after the original crash period began many of the homes that lost 25 percent (or even far more in many cases and in overinflated-valued regions around the country) have still not recovered or just barely recovered.

It helps to explain why so many people quickly despaired and chose to default on their mortgages and to simply give the house back to the bank lender and then to walk away free and clear. Ironically in many cases, their shattered credit history and associated credit rating would actually recover faster than the value of their severely underwater home and mortgage finally did.

Deed

A Deed refers to a legal document which allows for a real estate ownership transfer from one party to another. Within the document will always be the names of the new and old owners of the property as well as the legally binding description of said real estate. The document must be signed over by the individual who is selling the property to the buyer.

It is impossible to transfer ownership of a piece of real estate unless you have a document in writing. This is nearly always the deed. Interestingly enough, there is not simply one type of these deeds. There are quitclaim, warranty, grant, and transfer on death kinds of deeds in existence. Each of them has their own reason of use.

Quitclaim deeds are what many individuals regard as basic deeds. They simply transfer over any ownership stake an individual may have in a given property. These do not define the full percentage of the receiver's interest in the property however. They are often utilized by couples getting divorced. One of the aggrieved parties signs off on his or her full rights in the married couple's joint properties to the other party. This is particularly helpful when a lack of clarity exists on an interest in a property that one of the owners (like a spouse) has in his or her name. Quitclaims never absolve the forfeiting party from the co- responsibilities of the mortgage however.

These Quitclaim deeds are also employed when title searches discover that a prior owner or heir to an estate possesses a partial claim on the real estate in question. That individual is able to sign off on such a quitclaim deed in order to allow for the transfer of whatever interest remains to them in the said property.

Warranty deeds provide ownership transfer along with a good guarantee that the transferring party possesses clean title on the real estate. This means that the purchaser can have confidence in the property being completely free of ownership claims or liens. These deeds deliver a guarantee from the sellers that they will provide compensation to the purchasers should this pledge prove to be incorrect. It is also possible for warranty deeds to provide other guarantees that address other potential issues with the real estate transfer transaction.

Grant deeds are those kinds that imply certain pledges along with transferring the ownership of title to the property. These pledges might include that the title is not encumbered or has not previously transferred over to someone else.

Finally, TOD Transfer on Death deeds are much like regular formats of deeds. Their critical difference is that they only go into effect when the owner of the property in question dies. In other words, they permit property holders to will real estate to an heir without having to become involved in proceedings in probate court. Upon death, the deed-named beneficiary will immediately assume ownership of the real estate. This avoids any and all delays and probate paperwork.

Creating such TOD deeds is not any more difficult than completing normal deeds. The owner simply designates the beneficiary, signs said deed, has it notarized, and records it with the appropriate property records office for the given jurisdiction. Such deeds are permitted in 23 different states. These include Wyoming, Wisconsin, Washington, Virginia, South Dakota, Oregon, Oklahoma, Ohio, North Dakota, New Mexico, Nevada, Nebraska, Montana, Missouri, Minnesota, Kansas, Indiana, Illinois, Hawaii, Washington District of Columbia, Colorado, Arkansas, and Arizona.

Deeds are required by law to first be notarized (and sometimes also witnessed) before being filed in the area public records office. The appropriate local records office is typically called either a Land Registry Office, County Recorder's Office, or Register of Deeds. This office is typically located within the county courthouse.

Deed in Lieu of Foreclosure

A deed in lieu of foreclosure represents an alternative option to a standard foreclosure on a house. In this deed in lieu arrangement, the owner of the property decides to hand over the property in question to the lender on a completely voluntary basis. In exchange for agreeing to this, the lender cancels out the mortgage loan. The deed to the house becomes transferred from the owner to the lender. As part of this conciliatory arrangement, the mortgage lender guarantees that it will not start the foreclosure process on the owner. If there are any foreclosure actions that have already begun, the lender will also terminate these. It is up to the lender to decide if they will forgive any extra balance that the sale of the home does not cover.

There are some tax issues that can arise with a deed in lieu of foreclosure deal. One potential downside to this type of debt forgiveness involves the consequences of it with the IRS. Federal law in the United States requires creditors to file 1099C forms for tax purposes when they choose to forgive any loan balance that amounts to more than $600. This debt forgiveness is then considered to be income and it becomes a tax liability for the home owner.

Fortunately for many home owners during the financial crisis, Congress passed the Mortgage Forgiveness Debt Relief Act of 2007. This delivered tax relief on a number of loans that banks forgave in the years starting from 2007 till the end of 2013.

The main issue and advantage that a deed in lieu of foreclosure offers centers around this excess balance debt forgiveness. Anyone who enters into such a voluntary agreement should carefully review the contract to learn how the deficiency balance topic will be addressed. Sometimes the documents are not clear on this point.

In this case, the homeowner should take the deed in lieu document to a lawyer who specializes in property law. It is not inexpensive to have a lawyer review such a contract document. The money it can save the home owner in the future for signing a contract he or she does not understand and may suffer significantly from will make the fees seem reasonable by comparison.

There are a number of requirements in order for a deed in lieu of foreclosure to be accepted. First the house would have to be on the seller market for a minimum number of days. Ninety days is usual. There also may not be any liens on the house. The property typically could not be in the process of foreclosure already. Finally, the deed in lieu offer has to be voluntary on the part of the home owner.

Another option that can be pursued in place of this deed in lieu of foreclosure is a short sale. Short sales have the same requirements as do the deed in lieu arrangements with several additional stipulations. The home seller must be suffering from financial hardship. The home itself has to be offered at a reasonable price.

In an alternative short sale, the mortgage lender will consent to receiving a lesser amount from the sale than the remaining mortgage balance that the owner still owes. It is up to the bank and the contract if any additional balance which exists will be forgiven or not. The same tax issues apply if the lender agrees to forgive more than $600.

Deed of Priority

Deed of Priority refers to a deed or other form of contract where two or more creditors concur between themselves on the order that their security for a debtor in common will rank. In other words, they set out the rights which each of them will have pertaining to recovering the debts which the specific debtor in question owes them all should said debtor choose to default.

Many times in practice this phrase is interchanged with the similar term inter-creditor agreement. It is true that both kinds of documents look to arrange the order of precedence rank between a group of creditors. There are important differences between these two types of documents though. For one, the inter-creditor agreement is usually a more complicated document. It tends to detail equity and debt provider rights as well as the rights to obtain payments in advance of a debtor going insolvent and the rights to seize security.

Deeds of Priority are also referred to as Waiver Arrangements in Britain, and as Ranking Arrangements in Scotland. Both businesses and consumers have opportunities to source finance from multiple sources. Each lender will want some form of security with which to back the loan naturally. This might amount to any business assets or only specific ones. The second lender will also wish to obtain security in the form of some of the business assets regarding the loan they are issuing.

It is critical for every lender involved in the project, both original ones and new ones, to be aware of the different security arrangements which have already been made between the customer and earlier lenders. In other words, the various lenders will need someone to act as liaison between them so that each lender is able to ascertain and confirm its part of the secured assets, as well as its ranking for them. They will require such assurances before they actually issue the funds in the agreed upon loan.

There are a means by which they could attempt to effectively do this. One of them is the waiver arrangement. Another is using the deed of priority discussed in this article. The deed of priority is usually preferable since it spells out clearly and concisely the terms which pertain between each and every lender in the case of this specific borrower. It helps them all to understand how the various company or personal assets will be fairly and equitably distributed and shared out in the case of a default on one or more of their repayment agreements with the borrowing customer.

These scenarios will most commonly arise when a business already had a financing arrangement in place with a traditional bank. The business may then open negotiations with what is known as an alternative lender to borrow additional capital. Naturally this alternative lender will then want an arrangement hammered out with the other lender so that it can be sure of obtaining some level of collateral security over assets which are already pledged in part or whole to the original lender.

They will then sit down to fine tune the priority ranking of the various securities of the business, or to establish a release of assets from the existing security in play with the original lender. Paperwork must be drawn up, legalized, and signed off on by all lenders involved typically as swiftly as possible.

Fortunately for British- based businesses, there is a protocol in place to handle these matters. The British Bankers Association (or BBA) has compiled a PDF document called the "Deeds of Priority and Waivers: What You Need to Know as a Small or Medium Sized Business and What the Major Banks Are Committed to."

All of the major British banks have signed on to the terms of this protocol, making it far easier for British businesses to work out the deeds of priority arrangements so that they can obtain their supplementary financing from the second institutions.

Deed of Trust

A Deed of Trust refers to a critically important document which is associated with purchasing a house. Coupled with the promissory note, these are arguably the two most important documents which get signed in a closing on a home. The deed of trust proves to be the loan security. It is similarly the one which becomes recorded with public records in the local area governing jurisdiction. This deed can be numerous pages long.

There are three component parties to the deed of trust. The trustor is ultimately the borrower. The beneficiary proves to be the lender on the deal. The trustee is that third party entity that maintains the ownership of the title throughout the terms of the loan. These instruments will identify many important terms to the mortgage and the loan arrangements. Among these is the principal amount of the loan, the names of the various parties, and the property's legal description which ultimately secures the mortgage. It also details the mortgage requirements and provisions, the loan's maturity date and inception date, the legal proceedings, and the late fees associated with the account. Finally, the deed will cover alienation and acceleration clauses along with riders that pertain to clauses such as adjustable rate mortgages and prepayment penalties that may apply.

It is critically important to understand who or what the trustee is on a given mortgage. Mortgages themselves do not come with a trustee. Yet the deeds of trust do. This must always be a neutral third party which neither represents the interests of neither the lender nor the borrower. It would often be an entity or organization like the title company. Such a group will maintain the rights known as the "Power of Sale" should the borrower default. Once the deed has been paid off fully, the trustee will reconvey the property. The trustee has the duty to file the Notice of Default should the borrower default. Generally though, such a trustee will bring in another trustee to arrange the foreclosure terms in what is called a Substitution of Trustee.

In either case, following 90 day periods while the public records are updated and the subsequent 21 day publication in the major area circulating newspaper, the trustee has the rights to sell the property directly from the steps of the courthouse without undergoing standard court proceedings. Up to this point, the borrower could reclaim the property by catching up on all missed back payments and covering the fees the trustee has assumed to that point. After a trustee sells the property in the Trustee Sale, this is considered to be binding and final.

The promissory note should never be confused with the Deed of Trust. The deed secures both the debt and the property. The promissory note is further secured by the deed itself. This comprises the debt's evidence of existence. Besides this, the promissory note represents the borrower's promise to repay the mortgage debt. It will contain all applicable terms like payment obligations and interest rates. Though it is not usually recorded, this note will be stamped "paid in full" and given back to the appropriate borrower with the recorded Reconveyance Deed. It is the lender who holds the promissory note up to the point when the borrower fully repays the loan. Borrowers do receive copies of these important documents.

With Deeds of Trust and Promissory Notes, borrowers should thoroughly read both documents before signing them. It is critically essential to review a number of items covered by both documents. These include the all-important loan balance principal, the trustors' names spelling, the interest rate, the amount of monthly payments, address of the property in question, and any prepayment penalties associate with the mortgage itself.

Delinquent Rent

Delinquent Rent refers to rent that tenants pay their landlords late. This is called one of the two greatest frustrations for landlords in the renting process. The other one is handling tenants who vandalize a place. Making good on late or unpaid rent is a hassle for landlords that is almost always an expensive and time consuming process. There are various processes available to landlords for them to obtain their unpaid or late rents. These vary widely based on the state where the property lies, as each state has its own laws pertaining to rentals. The rental agreement also plays its part based on the provisions it contains.

Rental relationships were once arranged with mere handshakes, but that simpler time is now long gone forever. In today's complicated and litigious world, such business arrangements become specified by the law and in contracts instead of on a trust basis. In today's rental arrangements, the rental agreement governs the means of obtaining Delinquent Rent or unpaid balances. This is why it is so important to obtain a solid rent contract template before individuals become landlords and execute rental agreements for the first time.

Oral arrangements are never a good idea in these scenarios. This is because courts frown on enforcing them and they may even doubt their existence or validity. Well-defined lease contracts spell out each provision of the rental arrangements. This includes the amount of rent that has to be furnished and at what point said rent must be paid. Landlords who are unable to specify the precise date on which the rent must be paid will find they are often stymied in their subsequent late and unpaid rent collection endeavors.

It is similarly important for landlords to never agree to verbal alterations to a written out and executed contract. Verbal changes become hotly contested and debatable in law courts. They often will diminish the ability to collect on late rents which the written contract adequately specified. This is why instead the landlords must focus on writing in the maximum number of self help (for rental collection) avenues as the laws in a given state will permit.

In the majority of cases, the state laws provide for two different forms of dealing with unpaid and Delinquent Rent. The ones mentioned above are called self help remedies. These involve any methods a landlord may enforce without needing to make court appearances, file lawsuits, and involve judges. They can only include the relevant property code and state rental law provision allowances. Some of these so-called self help remedies include the ability to enforce liens on the personal property of the renter, to post a notice of eviction, and to physically engage in a lockout of the tenant by changing the locks on the property.

There are states that restrict the kinds of personal property that landlords may seize against Delinquent Rent or back rent. State contract law usually has provisions governing lockouts and eviction notices too. Landlords have to obey the contractual and state law requirements for both methods carefully. For example, shutting off electricity, water, and gas is typically not permitted by most states among the procedures for collecting late rent.

Eviction notices are often the most effective means of dealing with back rent. This is because the majority of tenants do not actually wish to be evicted forcefully by the sheriff from the property. The will generally respond to such a notice by paying any and all rent which they owe at this point.

When self help remedies do not resolve the situation, the small claims court is the place that handles the majority of landlord-tenant disputes. The landlord will have to pay filing fees in order to lodge a rent collection lawsuit. Tenants must be notified of the opening of such a rental dispute lawsuit. Every jurisdiction has its own regulations for the format of the notice which the landlord must provide to the tenant. Among these are in person notification, by fax, by mail, or other means of notification. Once a hearing is held before the judge, a judgment will typically be awarded for the rent that remains unpaid or delinquent.

Discount Fee

Discount fee refers to an upfront closing cost on a mortgage. This one time arrangement provides a mortgage borrower with the ability to enjoy lower mortgage rates than the general market offers. These discount points are often tax deductible. This is because the IRS counts these points as mortgage interest that is prepaid. The discount fee varies from one bank to another in how much it lowers the interest rate on the mortgage. Typically, a single discount point that a buyer pays in the closing will reduce the interest rate on the mortgage by 25 basis points, or .25%.

Mortgage lenders commonly quote their own current mortgage rates as two parts. In the first part, they provide the official mortgage rate which they are offering. In the second part they reveal the amount of discount fee that the borrower will need to pay to reach that rate. Generally speaking, the more points the home buyer pays, the lower the quote on the mortgage rate will become.

Ultimately the discount fee is a means of buying down the interest rate. This lowers the monthly payments. It is separate from origination points. These are costs that banks levy in order to prepare the mortgage loan.

Settlement statements may label this discount fee under another name. They can be termed mortgage rate buy down or discount points. These points carry a cost of 1% of the total size of the loan. With a $300,000 loan, a single point would cost $3,000. Half a point would amount to $1,500. A quarter point would equal $750.

The tax advantage of these discount points pertains to taxes a home buyer pays now. They are completely deductible in the year the borrower buys them. Individuals are not allowed to claim the full deduction on loans for home refinance. These must be spread out for the entire life of the refinance loan. This means that for a home owner who buys points for a 30 year refinance mortgage, he or she is able to claim 1/30 of the fees every year in tax deduction. For any borrower who decides to buy these points on a mortgage, it makes sense to discuss it with the tax advisor so that the deductions on federal income tax can be maximized.

The other reason that a home buyer would be interested in buying points is because it can lower the monthly payments and the total amount of money paid during the life of the mortgage loan. On a $100,000 loan a standard discount point would reduce payments by $14 each month for every $1,000 spent. This leads to a breakeven time frame of 71 months.

In order for buying points to make sense, the mortgage borrower has to decide how long he or she will likely hold the house or the mortgage. If the owner plans to sell the house in less than this amount of time, or he or she will refinance the loan sooner, then paying for points becomes a waste of money. If an owner will hold a mortgage for more than the six years in this example, then the savings over the remaining 24 years of the mortgage can be substantial.

Freddie Mac keeps statistics on average mortgage loans and points. In the year 2015, the average fixed rate loan came with .6 discount points. With the average ARM adjustable rate mortgage, .5 discount points came in the contract. The exact amount of an interest rate break that a point carries depends on the bank in question. Some banks also do not give multiples of .25% interest rate breaks on each point the borrower purchases.

Discount Mortgage Broker

A discount mortgage broker is one who claims that the lender is paying his or her fees. These mortgage brokers shop for competitive loan deals on the behalf of consumers looking for mortgages. Upfront mortgage brokers by contrast are ones that spell out exactly the fees they will receive from the borrower. Their charges are part of the closing costs of the loan.

The phrase discount mortgage broker gives the connotation that the individual is offering services for a reduced price. This is usually the opposite of what they do. Discount brokers usually charge higher fees. The borrower is not able to recognize this much of the time because the fees are buried in the higher interest rate which he or she will pay over the life of the loan. When the borrower pays in the rate, the payment becomes extended over years instead of a single upfront fee.

Lenders do not ever truly pay the fees of mortgage brokers. Borrowers always front them in one of two ways. With upfront brokers, the borrower pays the costs upfront in cash when it is time for the mortgage loan to close. This makes the fee for the broker a part of the closing costs.

The other way is for the borrower to pay a higher rate of interest to the lender. The lender then covers the broker cost during the closing in exchange for the higher interest rate. This means that the fee would not be a closing cost for the borrower. The borrower is still paying the fee. He or she is paying it instead each month of the loan in the form of a higher mortgage payment.

A discount mortgage broker prefers to have the fee paid by the lender in the closing. The reason for this is that resistance from the borrower to the fees is considerably less when the borrower does not understand the way it works. Consumers are usually extremely focused on the cash which they must come up with at closing than they are on payments they will make in the future.

The disclosure forms which are required do not clearly spell out rebates that the broker receives. The home buyers know all too well how much these fees are when they pay it personally at closing. They often have little idea of how much the broker is charging and receiving when they pay it from the interest rate.

This is why a discount mortgage broker is always looking to receive its compensation completely in the form of rebates from the lender. There is nothing illegal or unethical when borrowers pay their brokers via a higher interest rate in lieu of a cash payment. Transparency would argue that a home buyer should at least be able to make the choice intentionally.

Some borrowers can actually benefit from paying the discount mortgage broker through the rate and rebate. In the cases where the home buyers will not pay this greater rate for too long, then it can save them money over the upfront out of pocket mortgage broker fees. For individuals who will keep their mortgage a greater amount of time, it saves them money to pay the broker directly at closing. This is provided they have the cash available.

Discount Points

Discount points are also sometimes known as simply points. They represent a type of interest that is paid in advance. A single discount point is equivalent to one percent of the total loan amount. Through charging borrowers points, lenders boost their loan's yield to a total that is higher than the expressed interest rate.

Borrowers are able to give a bank or lender payment as a way of lowering the loan's interest rates. The up front sum of money gives them a lower monthly payment. With every point that a borrower buys, their loan's rate commonly falls by .125 percent. A buyer paying for points is not without risk. At some time within the life of the loan, the cost of the money given to lower the rate of interest will equal out to the money that you saved in being able to make lower amount loan payments because of the loan's better interest rate.

Should you refinance the loan or sell the house in advance of attaining this break even point, then you will actually take a loss on the transaction. On the other hand, if you hold on to the property and accompanying mortgage for a greater amount of time than the break even, then you will actually save money on the purchase.

It goes without saying that the longer amount of time that you hold the property mortgage and financing with the bought discount points, the better this money used for the points actually rewards you. At the same time, a person who plans on purchasing the property and then selling it or refinancing it quickly will only lose money by not simply paying the higher rate of interest on the loan in lieu of buying points.

Discount points can also be bought to help you qualify for loans. If the loan qualification basis is grounded in your monthly loan payment against your monthly income, then you may only be capable of getting approval by buying the discount points to lower the rate of interest which will result in the lower monthly payment that your approval requires.

Discount points should not be confused with broker fees or origination fees. Discount points only serve to lower the interest rates. Origination fees are those that the lender charges for creating and closing the loan. They could sometimes be a different name for lowering the interest rate as well.

Borrowers who will stay in the house for a longer period of time should definitely consider buying points. Lower interest rates will pay off in savings over time. Any changes in the fees and costs for the loan will be shown to you in the last good faith estimate that the lender provides.

Sometimes when you buy points, you may be able to get a no closing cost loan. This usually happens when the bank is getting a premium interest rate. As their fee is made off of a higher starting interest rate on the note, it can be utilized to cover the closing costs.

Discount Rate

The term discount rate actually has several meanings. Where interest rates and banks are concerned, the discount rate proves to be the actual interest rate that central banks charge their member depositing institutions. When these banks choose to borrow funds from the central bank or the Federal Reserve as their lender of last resort, then this is the rate that they will be required to pay them as interest.

Besides this, the discount rate can refer to the annual effective discount rate in investments. This rate turns out to be the yearly interest divided up by the capital that includes the interest. The rate provides a lower value than does the interest rate. The value following a year delay would be the nominal value in this case. The upfront value is this nominal value less a discount. This annual effective discount rate is commonly utilized for financial instruments that are like Treasury Bills.

For businesses, the discount rate is important as they are making critical decisions regarding their profits and what to do with them. When it is time to contemplate whether to purchase new equipment pieces or to instead return the profits to the share holders, this discount rate is helpful. If all else is equal, then the company will only elect to purchase the equipment if it returns a greater profit to the share holders at a future point.

The share holder discount rate would then be the dollar total that share holders expect to receive in the future so that they would rather have the company purchase the equipment now instead of return the profits to them now. Share price data is utilized to figure up the discount rate for estimating share holders' preferences. This is called the capital asset pricing model. Businesses commonly use this discount rate when they make choices regarding buying equipment by using the net present value in the decision making process.

This discount rate proves to be the weighted average cost of capital. It shows the cash flow risk. The discount rate can also be used by companies to show two different things. It demonstrates the time value that money has, or the risk free rate. Investors generally prefer cash now than cash that they must wait for, meaning that businesses have to compensate them by making them wait for it. The discount rate also establishes a risk premium. This proves to be the additional return that investors want as payment for the possibility that they might not ever see this money if the cash flow is not there in the future.

Down Payment

A down payment is an upfront amount that is given as a portion of the price on a purchase of large ticket items such as houses or cars. These are given in cash or by check when the contract is signed. The balance of the sum due is then given as a loan.

Down payments are principally intended to make sure that the bank or other type of lending institution is capable of recovering the remaining balance that is owed on a loan should the borrower choose to default. In transactions of real estate, the underlying asset becomes collateral that secures the associated loan against potential default.

Should the borrower not repay the loan as agreed, then the bank or institutional lender is allowed to sell this collateral asset and keep enough of the money received to pay off the rest of the loan along with the interest and fees included. In these cases, down payments decrease the exposure risk of the lender to an amount that is smaller than the collateral's value. This increases the chance of the bank getting the entire principal loaned out back should the borrower default.

The amount of such a down payment therefore impacts the lender's exposure to the loan and protects against anything that might lessen the collateral's value. This includes profits that are lost from the point of the final payment to the final collateral sale. The making of this down payment assures a lender that the borrower has capital available for long term investments, further proof that the finances of the borrower are able to afford the item in the first place. Should a borrower not successfully pay down the full loan amount, then he or she will lose the entire down payment.

Down payments on houses bought in the United States typically range anywhere from 3.5% to 20% of the full purchase amount. The Federal Housing Administration helps first time borrowers to pay merely 3.5% as a down payment. In the excesses of the years leading up to the financial collapse of 2007, many banks were making loans with no down payments. On car purchases, these amounts of down payments might be in the range of from 3% to 13%.

Dual Index Mortgage

Dual Index Mortgages are products of Latin American countries. They are especially popular in places like Mexico that have experienced significant inflation levels historically. These kinds of mortgages permit borrowers to buy houses even when a substantial amount of inflation risk exists. They are not and have never been offered in the United States, though they have been compared to ARM Adjustable Rate Mortgages.

Dual Index Mortgages do show some similarities to the American Adjustable Rate Mortgages. Such ARMs have always been in demand in places in the U.S. that are more expensive to buy houses. As with these types of loans, the dual index ones provide the borrower with lower early monthly payments that will cause negative amortization to occur. This means that the loan balances will rise for many months before they gradually begin to decline.

With Dual Index Mortgages, the rate that the lender earns is indexed. This means that the rate becomes adjusted at periodically set time intervals. The banks are able to adjust the rate on the loan according to the market rate changes.

The borrowers suffer from other aspects of the Dual Index Mortgages. On the positive side, the first payments are designed to be affordable for the borrowers to be able to make. The payments and the interest rates are not the same with these loans. This is where they are significantly different from American ARMs. The payment could be figured at 5% for example while the interest rate due to the lender is 25% or even higher. The substantial difference between these two rates becomes an add on to the loan balance in the form of negative amortization. This means that it may be a great number of years before the balance on this kind of loan starts to go down.

The actual payment amount is determined based on a salaries and wages index. This amount will change each month. The reason the Dual Index Mortgages are dual is because the payments adjust with the income index at the same time as the interest rate adjust to the interest rate index. The hope with these mortgages is that the payment made by the borrower will one day reach the level where it more than covers the interest rate so that the loan balance can decline finally.

The problem with this is that salaries and wages may not match inflation increases in Mexico and other Latin American countries. This would cause the borrower payments to not increase quickly enough for the loan principal to be paid down. In this case, there are remaining unpaid principal balances at the end of the loan terms. Some lenders in Mexico have been willing to underwrite Dual Index Mortgages where they take on this significant risk. The majority of them receive insurance from the government of Mexico. If there are unpaid remaining balances, the government will absorb the losses.

Besides these Dual Index Mortgages, Mexico has also experimented with some other kinds of home loans. One of these is known as the PLAM, or Price Level Adjusted Mortgage. These are less common than the dual index types.

Electronic Funds Transfer (EFT)

EFT is the usual acronym for Electronic Funds Transfer. This program refers to the all-electronic money transfer processed out of one bank account and into another. This could be done within a single bank or over a number of different and often intermediary financial institutions. Computer systems handle these transactions entirely unaided by the intervention of human bank personnel. There are actually many different names for EFTs. Within the United States, they are often called e-checks or even electronic checks.

The phrase relates to a wide range of varying payment systems. Some of these are bank debit card or other credit card payments which a cardholding customer initiates voluntarily at a store or merchant, direct debit payments in which the firm directly debits the bank account of the consuming customers in payment for their services or goods, and payer initiated direct deposit. Other examples of this EFTs include wire transfers done utilizing the SWIFT banking international network, private currency transactions that deal with electronic money storage, and online banking electronic bill pay services that are often delivered via Electronic Funds Transfer or alternatively by using paper based checks.

Government agencies within the United States have also taken to utilizing Electronic Funds Transfers in recent years. The federal government touts them as an efficient and often practical means of collecting money and similarly paying it out electronically without having to engage in the time consuming and wasteful process of resorting to relying on paper based checks, purchasing and obtaining stamps, and generally considerable processing and mailing time lags. They encourage government agencies to adopt this payment technology if they have not already.

As the Federal Government has recently noted, EFT payments are secure, safe, and efficient. They are also less costly to utilize than any form of paper check collection or payment process. As a clear and concrete example, it helps to consider a real world case. The federal government calculates that it requires a full $1.03 in order to make a payment via a check. This represents over a dollar for a single payment transaction. Naturally this cost adds up considerably when agencies are engaging in millions of individual payments per month. Compare these costs with the government expenses for running payments via electronic formats. Every time the government enters and initiates an electronic funds transfer, it only pays the equivalent of .105 dollars (or slightly more than a single dime) per individual transaction.

In order to participate in either the government's version of EFT or any bank's version of electronic funds transfer, individuals must first sign up for the payment platform. Nowadays, all federal benefits have been switched over to and must be paid out electronically, which makes this more critical and timely to do now than ever before. For any person who receives any kind of these benefits, including SSI Supplemental Security Income, Social Security payments, civil service retirement payments, Veteran's benefits, railroad retirement payments, or military federal retirement, all benefits must be received by electronic funds transfer in order to be processed and paid out each month.

There are still other benefits which both the federal government and other private parties pay utilizing Electronic Funds Transfers. The Federal government calls its various benefit payment programs either Direct Express or Go Direct. Private parties and banks utilize a range of different labels and names for these various privately run programs.

Escrow

Escrow is a concept that relates to a sum of money that is kept by an uninvolved third party for the two parties involved in a given transaction. In the U.S., this escrow is most commonly involved where real estate mortgages are concerned. Here is it utilized for the payment of insurance and property tax during the mortgage's life.

When you place your money into such an escrow account, an escrow agent who is a neutral third party holds it. This agent works on behalf of both the borrower and home lender. The escrow agent's job in the transaction is to act as the principal parties instruct him or her. As all transaction terms are fulfilled, the money is then released. These escrow accounts may be a part of transactions ranging from small purchases affected on online auction sites to building projects that total in the multiple millions of dollars.

Escrow is utilized in these property transactions when it is time for your mortgage to close. At this point, the borrower's lender will commonly insist that you establish an escrow account for paying for both home owner's insurance and property taxes. You are required to make a first deposit to the account. After this, you make payments into the account each month. Typically, these are simply a part of your monthly mortgage payments. When it is time for your insurance premiums and taxes to be paid, your escrow agent then releases the funds.

The concept behind this escrow is to give your lender peace of mind and protection that your insurance and taxes are both paid in a timely manner. Should you not pay your property taxes, the city might place a lien on this house, making it hard for the bank to sell it if they needed to. Similarly, if a fire burned down the house and the insurance premiums had not been paid, the bank would not have any underlying collateral for the mortgage anymore.

You the borrower also benefit from this escrow account. It allows you to stretch out your taxes and insurance costs over the course of the entire year's twelve payments. As an example, your annual property taxes might prove to be $3,000, with a yearly insurance cost of $600. This would mean that when spread out over twelve even payments, the escrow costs would amount to only $300 each month.

The nice thing about escrow accounts and payments is that they come with an included safeguard built in. Should you miss a single payment, then the responsible lender is still capable of paying the accounts in a timely manner. The U.S. Federal law actually stops these lenders from storing up in excess of two months' worth of payments in escrow. As insurance and tax amounts will vary a little from one year to the next, the lender will have to examine and make adjustments to your annual escrow payments.

Eviction

Eviction involves the forced removal of a rental tenant from a landlord's rental property. Other terms that convey the same or a similar meaning include repossession, summary possession, and ejection. Eviction proves to be the term most commonly utilized in landlord and tenant communications. Evictions can not simply happen without going through a legal process that could include an eviction lawsuit.

A notice must first be given to the tenant by the landlord. This is most often referred to as the notice to vacate or notice to quit. It has to be delivered to a tenant in advance of beginning official legal eviction procedures. In most cases, the tenant will then receive somewhere from three to ten days to address the issue causing eviction. These offenses likely are caused by either a failure to pay the rent in a timely manner or contractual breach of the lease for something like have a pet.

Should the tenant refuse to leave the property in question after the expiration of the notice to quit, then the landlord next provides the tenant with a complaint. These complaints mandate that the tenant in question will have to go to court. If the tenant refuses to appear at the court date or does not provide an answer to the complaint, then the landlord is able to seek a default judgment, in which he or she automatically wins the case. A tenant response should include his or her side of the story as well as defense that could include the tenant not being provided with repairs that the lease stipulates.

Following an appropriate answer, trial dates are determined. With the issues being dependent on time, these cases are commonly hurried through the system. Should a judge back up a tenant, then the tenant is allowed to stay, although he or she would have to pay back due rent. Should the landlord be victorious, then the tenant receives a little window to move out of the property before being forcefully evicted. This is commonly only a week, though with a stay of execution, the tenant could be given more time.

Some jurisdictions permit a tenant to have a right to redemption in the eviction process. This would allow a tenant to cancel a pending eviction and to stay in the rented property by catching up immediately on the back rent along with other appropriate fees. These rights become waived should the tenant constantly be late in paying the rent.

Finally, after a tenant has lost his or her eviction lawsuit, the tenant is commonly given a particular number of days in which to abandon the property. This has to be done before other repercussions occur. Sometimes the tenant will be told to leave immediately.

Landlords are given writs of possession by the court after the tenant has lost the lawsuit and still refused to leave. These writs of possession are then turned over to a law enforcement officer. Such an officer would then put up an official notice for a tenant to depart the property before the date on which the officer will return to forcibly remove the tenant. If the tenant is not gone when the officer returns, he is permitted to take the tenant and anyone else on the property and remove them. They will be allowed to take away their possessions or place them in storage before the property is given back to the landlord.

Fair Housing Act

The Fair Housing Act of 1968 is officially known as Title VIII from the Civil Rights Act of 1968. It makes it illegal to discriminate with regards to renting, selling, or financing homes or apartments. No one may consider color, race, sex, religion, or national origin in these activities.

Congress amended the Fair Housing Act of 1968 with the Fair Housing Amendments Act in 1988. These amendments expanded the rulings of the original act in a number of important ways. No one was permitted to discriminate with housing because of an individual's disability or based on their family status. This meant that home sellers or renters could not disallow families with pregnant women or who had children less than 18 years of age living with them.

To prevent disability discrimination, the act included construction and design accessibility rules for some multifamily homes. Those that were to be occupied initially after March 13, 1991 had to comply with the accessibility provisions for disabled people.

The amendments also created new means of enforcing and administering the rules. HUD Housing and Urban Development attorneys were now able to take cases to administrative law judges for victims of such housing discrimination. The jurisdiction of the Justice Department became expanded and revised in such a way that it could file suits in Federal district courts for discrimination victims.

HUD has been tasked with the principal responsible to administer the Fair Housing Act of 1968 since the government adopted it. Thanks to the amendments in 1988, the department has become substantially more involved in enforcing the provisions. This is because the newly protected families and disabled brought many new complaints. The department also had to move beyond investigating and conciliating. They were tasked with mandatory enforcing the rules.

Any complaint regarding the Fair Housing Act of 1968 that individuals file with HUD becomes investigated. The FHEO Fair Housing and Equal Opportunity office handles this responsibility. When complaints can not be resolved voluntarily, the FHEO decides if there is sufficient evidence for a reasonable case of discrimination in housing practices. If they find reasonable cause, then HUD issues a Determination and Charge of Discrimination to the complaint parties. Hearings are next scheduled in front of a law judge for the HUD administration. Either the complaining party or the accused can terminate this procedure to instead have the matter resolved in Federal courts.

At this point, the Department of Justice assumes HUD's responsibility for the aggrieved party's complaints. They act as counsel that seeks to resolve the charges. The matter then becomes a civil case. In either the case of the HUD law judge hearing or the civil action held in the courts, the U.S. Court of Appeals can review the outcome.

The Fair Housing Act of 1968 proved to be historic as the final major act in the civil rights movement legislation. Despite this, housing remained segregated throughout much of the United States for decades. During the thirty years from 1950 through 1980, America's urban centers' black population grew from 6.1 million up to 15.3 million people.

At the same time, white Americans continuously abandoned the cities in favor of the suburbs. With them went a great number of the jobs that the black population needed to communities where they did not find welcome. The result of this ongoing trend caused urban America to be filled with ghettos. These are the communities inside the American inner cities where many minority populations live. They have been dogged by consistently high crime, unemployment, drug use, and other social problems.

Fannie Mae

Fannie Mae is the acronym for the FNMA Federal National Mortgage Association. This entity is a GSE Government Sponsored Enterprise along with brother organization Freddie Mac. It became a publicly traded company in 1968. This home lending giant proves to be the largest mortgage financing provider anywhere in the United States. As such, it funds significantly more mortgages than any competing company or entity. It ensures that homebuyers, homeowners, and renters around the U.S. all can obtain financing options which they can afford.

As the GSE became established in 1938, it has provided funding for the housing market of the country for over 75 years. Franklin D. Roosevelt's New Deal established the company in the midst of the Great Depression. This is why the mission of the company is to aid individuals in purchasing, renting, or refinancing a home whether economic times in the country are good or bad.

The company's explicit purpose is to boost the size of the secondary mortgage market. They do this when they securitize mortgages and package them into MBS mortgage backed securities. This process returns the mortgage loaned money to lenders who are then able to reinvest this money into additional lending. It also acts to grow the numbers of lending institutions who are issuing mortgages. This ensures that there are more than just savings and loan associations making local loans for housing.

The model worked well until between 2003 and 2004. At this point the subprime mortgages crisis started. It began when the mortgage market turned away from the GSEs like Freddie Mac and Fannie Mae and began to migrate rapidly to unregulated MBS Mortgage Backed Securities that major investment banks put together. This shift to private MBSs caused the GSEs to lose their control over and ability to monitor mortgages in the country.

Increased competition between the investment banks and the GSEs reduced the power and market share of the government mortgage backers further and boosted the mortgage lenders at their expense. This radical change in the way mortgages were overseen and made caused the underwriting standards for mortgages to dangerously decline. It turned out to be one of the major reasons for the ensuing mortgage and financial crises.

The situation became so severe at Fannie Mae by 2008 that the FHFA Federal Housing Finance Agency had to get directly involved. FHFA Director James Lockhart on September 7, 2008 placed both this organization and Freddie Mac under FHFA conservatorship. This proved to be among the most dramatic and far reaching government involvements in free enterprise financial markets for literally decades.

Among Lockhart's first actions, he fired both companies' boards of directors and CEOs. He then made the companies issue a new class of common stock warrants and senior preferred stock to Treasury for 79.9% of both GSEs. Those who had been holding either preferred or common stock in either entity before the conservatorship began saw the value of their shares massively decrease. All prior shares' dividends became suspended to try to hold up the mortgage backed securities' and company debt values. FHFA pledged that it had no intentions of liquidating the GSEs.

Since 2009, Fannie Mae has made great strides in its business of helping make housing work better for individuals and families. They have injected trillions of dollars into the mortgage markets in lending liquidity. This has gone a long way to helping the housing markets and overall economy to recover.

The company has also gone back to high quality eligibility and underwriting standards. In the first quarter of 2016, they have extended $115 billion in mortgage credit that has allowed for 210,000 homes to be purchased and 256,000 mortgages to be refinanced. They also financed the construction of 161,000 multifamily rental units.

Federal Housing Finance Agency (FHFA)

The Federal Housing Finance Agency is a government regulating agency. They are independent and responsible for overseeing several agencies within the secondary mortgage market. These include Freddie Mac, Fannie Mae, and the Federal Home Loan Banks. They work to keep these critical government sponsored organizations, along with the entire American housing financial system, in good health.

As such, the FHFA labors constantly to build up and safeguard the secondary mortgage markets in the United States. They do this through their leadership in and delivering excellent research, dependable data, strong supervision, and pertinent policies. The three government sponsored entities of Freddie Mac, Fannie Mae, and the Federal Home Loan Bank system together deliver over $5.5 trillion in financial institutions and mortgage markets funding throughout the United States.

The FHFA helps to keep this all possible by providing their independent regulation and careful oversight of these vital mortgage markets. Besides this, they are also the conservator of both Freddie Mac and Fannie Mae since the financial crisis and Great Recession that began in 2007-2008 wreaked havoc on the two giant government sponsored agencies along with the housing market they guaranteed.

The Federal Housing Finance Agency is concerned with creating a better market of secondary mortgages for the country's future. To this effect, they are working on a sequence of strategies and initiatives to boost the housing financial system in the future. Among these new ideas is the construction of a new and improved database called the Common Securitization Platform. This will have dual roles. It will take the presently outdated infrastructures and modernize them. It will also allow for the possibilities of other players in the market choosing to utilize this same infrastructure.

The FHFA considers itself to be in a partnership. They strive alongside the entities they regulate to keep home ownership alive and affordable through a variety of programs. These include the HARP Home Affordable Refinance Program and the HAMP Home Affordable Modification Program. The two programs deliver significant and tangible aid to both communities and their homeowners. So far such programs have assisted literally millions of home owning Americans to keep or stay in their houses.

The FHFA does not have a long history. It is a new organization that grew out of the housing market collapse and Great Recession. President Obama signed the Housing and Economic Recovery Act of 2008 to create the Federal Housing Finance Agency back on July 30, 2008.

The ongoing mission of the FHFA is to make certain that the government sponsored enterprises for housing function in a manner that is both economically viable and safe. This is so that they can continue to provide a dependable source of both funds and liquidity for investment in communities and the financing of home purchases. As part of this, they envision a housing financial system that is stable, dependable, and liquid for both the present and the future.

The FHFA values four virtues. They prize excellence in all areas of their work. The organization appreciates respect for their team members, resources, and the information they collect. They value integrity and commit themselves to the greatest possible professional and moral standards. The group also encourages diversity in all of their business dealings and employment arrangements, as well as in the entities which they regulate and for whom they are the conservator.

FHFA is also an important member group of the Financial Stability Oversight Council. Chief among their tasks is to identify financial stability risks in the U.S., to respond to rising threats to the American financial system, and to encourage discipline in the market. They serve on this council with fellow members that include The Federal Reserve governors, CFTC, FDIC, Comptroller of the Currency, SEC, and Treasury Department.

Fixed Rate Mortgage

Fixed Rate Mortgages are products for mortgage loans that the FHA, or Federal Housing Administration, first created. In this type of mortgage, the interest rates in effect on the mortgage note stay at the same level during the entire life of the loan. This stands in stark contrast to loans where the interest rates are adjustable, or floating. There are also hybrid types of loans that involve fixed rates for a portion of the loan's life.

Fixed rate mortgages will have monthly payments that must be made to keep current on the mortgage. Besides the monthly payment there are property taxes and property insurance costs. These are typically set up in escrow accounts. With such escrow amounts, these are likely to change every so often. Still, the main share of the payments, which are associated with interest and principal on the mortgage, will stay the same.

Figuring up the monthly payments with fixed rate mortgages is relatively easy. You will have to acquire three pieces of data to do so. These are the interest rate with compounding of interest period, mortgage term, and amount of loan.

Fixed rate mortgages are also known by their nickname of plain vanilla mortgages. They have this moniker because of how simple they are for borrowers to understand. Such fixed rate mortgages do not entail the many risks and perils associated with adjustable rate mortgages that include pre set teasing rates or Adjustable Rate Mortgages. As such, Fixed rate mortgage default rates and foreclosure rates are commonly far lower than are these more experimental and risky mortgage products.

Several terms are commonly associated with Fixed Rate Mortgages. These include the fully indexed rate and the term. Fully indexed rates are the interest rate index plus the margin charged by the lender. Such a fully indexed rate proves to be the actual interest rate for the loan's entire life.

The term represents the amount of time that the fixed rate loan covers. This is not the same thing as the number of payments. Thirty year terms might have thirty payments if you were on an annual payment plan, or it might alternatively have 360 payments on a more usual monthly payment plan

The most popular and proven form of home loans and mortgage products within the United States are undoubtedly these fixed rate mortgages. Among the various mortgage terms that can be acquired, the most prevalent ones are either thirty year or fifteen year mortgages. Both shorter and longer time frames can be had with fixed rate mortgages.

These days, even forty and fifty year mortgages are presently offered. They are especially utilized in places with housing prices that are exceptionally high, as thirty year mortgage terms do not prove to be affordable for the average income family in such scenarios.

In contrast to fixed rate mortgages are various other types. These include graduated payment mortgages, balloon payment mortgages, and interest only mortgages. These unusual other types of mortgages commonly get borrowers into trouble, which is why they are not nearly so popular as are the fixed rate mortgages.

Fixer-Upper

Fixer-Upper is a term that is commonly associated with real estate property, such as houses, that need some significant repair and renovation work. Although these kinds of houses might be lived in despite their present condition, they usually want redesign, reconstruction, or redecoration of some form. Depending on how much repair or renovation work they require, fixer-upper's can be major projects that require significant investments of time and money.

Fixer-Upper's commonly result from houses that have not been taken care of or properly maintained. Because of this, they tend to possess market values that are lower than comparable houses found in the same locale. Fixer-Upper's can be discovered in the majority of communities, even in neighborhoods whose housing prices are not depressed.

Fixer-Upper's commonly prove to be very popular with buyers who act as investors in houses. They want to acquire the property cheaply so that they can repair it and increase its likely real estate value in order to acquire a nice profit on the investment. These projects as investments have gained greatly in popularity as a result of various do it yourself types of renovation shows that are all about home improvement. Many times in downturns in the real estate market, such as the one that has been ongoing since 2007, the interest in fixer-upper's declines.

There is a danger with Fixer-upper's for many buyers who think to improve and then flip them, or resell the house for profits. This is simply that they do not realize how much time and money will be required of them in repairing the house in question. Making a house salable will require addressing not only relatively simple cosmetic issues, but also potentially structural or service problems. When the plumbing or foundation is in need of major repairs or replacing, the work involved commonly turns out to be very expensive and needs professional contractors.

This is why determining if a Fixer-upper is a viable and worthy investment requires some experience and work. First, you will have to determine for how much the typical house in the neighborhood is selling. It is also wise to know what makes the most desirable houses in the neighborhood so in demand and how much they cost. Real estate agents can be helpful in this respect.

If you decide to pursue buying a Fixer-upper, then you should be watching for the truly cosmetic Fixer-upper's. These only require more basic improvements such as wallpaper, paint, new appliances, some landscape work, and possibly new window and floor coverings. Houses that look run down and require substantial structural repairs can be very dangerous and should be avoided. Houses that are priced too reasonably usually have a reason for this. Intelligent buyers should learn why this is the case before they commit their money.

The best strategy is to find the house that is the least wanted in the best neighborhood possible. The house and estimated repair cost must both be within your budget. Once at full fair market value, such a property should pay you back handsomely.

Foreclosure

Foreclosures represent houses or commercial properties that have been seized by a bank or other mortgage lender. These properties are then sold to recoup mortgage loan losses after an owner and borrower has not made the payments as promised in the mortgage agreement.

Foreclosure is also the legal procedure in which the lender gets a court order for the termination of the mortgagor's right of redemption. This is the case since most lenders have security interests in the house from the borrower. The borrower will secure the mortgage using the house as the collateral.

Borrowers fall into home foreclosure for several reasons, most of which could not be predicted in advance. Owner might have been let go from their job or forced to take a job transfer to another state. They might have suffered from medical problems that prevented them from working. They might have gone through a divorce and split up assets. They could have been overwhelmed by too many bills. Whatever the reason, they are no longer able to make their promised monthly mortgage payments.

Foreclosures represent potential opportunities for investors. They may be purchased directly with a seller in advance of a bank completing foreclosure proceedings. Many investors who concentrate on foreclosures prefer to deal with the owners directly. They have to be aware of many laws pertaining to foreclosures, which are different in every state. For example, while in some states home owners can stay in their properties for a full year after defaulting on payments, while in others, they have fewer than four months in advance of the trustee sale.

Practically all states also allow a redemption period for the delinquent homeowner. This simply means that a seller possesses an irrevocable ability to catch up on back payments and interest in order to retain ownership of the house. The owner will likely be required to pay any foreclosure costs experienced by the bank up to that point.

Another means of purchasing a foreclosure home is to buy it at the Trustee's Sale. When this means is pursued, it is better to bid on a house that allows you to look it over in advance of putting up an offer. This is helpful so that you can determine how many repairs will be needed to make it salable and even possibly habitable. It is also worth knowing if the occupants are still living in the house and will have to be forcefully evicted. The process of going through an eviction can be both expensive and time consuming.

Many Trustee Sales will have certain rules in common that have to be followed for a foreclosure house to be purchased. They may demand sealed bids. They could require you to demonstrate your proof of financial qualifications. They might similarly insist on you putting up a significant earnest money deposit. Many of them will state that the property is being purchased in its present condition, or as is.

Freddie Mac

Freddie Mac is a semi-private company that Congress chartered in 1970. They created the entity to offer stability, liquidity, and affordable prices for the country and its housing markets. They have grown to be responsible for the home purchases of one out of four buyers.

Besides this the company is also among the biggest financing sources for multifamily housing in the nation. From 2009 to 2016, the company has dispersed mortgage market funding that amounts to over $2.5 trillion. This has enabled in excess of 13 million American families to refinance, purchase, or rent a home in that time frame.

In 1970 Congress was seeking to stabilize the mortgage markets of the country. They wanted to grow and improve opportunities for rental housing that was affordable and for home buying. Because of this, Freddie Mac's mission has always been to bring stability, liquidity, and affordability to the national housing market in the United States. They do this in a variety of ways. The company helps the secondary mortgage market. They buy both mortgage securities and mortgage loans outright as investments. They then package and sell these as guaranteed mortgage securities known as PCs. In this secondary market, there are entities which buy and sell mortgages as complete loans or as mortgage securities. Freddie Mac never makes loans to home owners directly themselves.

Because of the collapse of the mortgage backed securities markets in 2007 and 2008 and its impact on their finances, the company is now being run under conservatorship. The FHFA Federal Housing Finance Agency oversees their business to make sure loans are carefully scrutinized and securitized. They want to avoid the mistakes of the financial crisis becoming repeated here.

Freddie Mac operates in three main business areas to ensure that a continuous supply of mortgage funding goes through to the housing markets in the country. They make rental housing and home buying more affordable through their single family credit guarantee business, their multifamily business, and their investment business. They utilize all three of these to promote financing for affordable housing.

The single family line is essentially a recycling operation. They work with securitizing mortgages so that the entity is able to provide funding to millions of different home loans annually. This securitization proves to be the means where they buy up different loans lenders have made and then package these up into various mortgage securities. They then sell these on the worldwide capital markets. The money from the sale of these securities they next funnel back to the lenders. In this way home loan operations have sufficient mortgage money for lending.

The company is also interested in supporting renters as well. This is the role of their multifamily business. In this line, the outfit cooperates with a group of lenders to help finance the construction of various apartment buildings throughout the United States. The lenders make the loans and Freddie Mac buys them to package and resell. This way the lenders receive back the proceeds so they can issue more loans. This is a critical line as multifamily loans prove to be a few million dollars each and require unique underwriting from one property to the next.

Their investment business actually purchases some of their own mortgage backed securities which they and other financial entities like Fannie Mae guarantee. This portfolio further invests into individual loans which they guarantee but choose not to securitize. By bidding on some of their own securities, the investment business and portfolio serves the markets. It gives these mortgage backed securities greater liquidity and offers more funding for mortgages. They do this by issuing their own debt which creates net income for the company after they pay their interest to the bond holders.

Good Debt

Good debt is debt that benefits a person or business to carry. Such good debts demonstrate both the creditworthiness and the responsibility of a borrower. They also create a good base to build on in the future. There are many examples of good debt, which stands in contrast to bad debt.

Good debts are typically those debts that are taken on to acquire an item or investment that only grows in value with time. Examples of this include things like real estate loans, schooling loans, home mortgages, business debt, and passive income investments. Each of these items could provide a significant and real advantage with time. Real estate could increase in value and be resold for profits.

Higher education commonly leads to greater amounts of earnings. Loans on homes are commonly wonderful for building credit and provide properties that serve as excellent collateral. Loans for businesses may result in profits earned from trade and sales. It is important to note that cars and other items are not included in these lists. This is simply because they lose value the moment that they are purchased and driven away.

Bad debts in contrast are those that result in higher interest rates and considerable deprecation of the items purchased with time. Goods that are for short time frame use and bought on credit are commonly considered to be bad debts. Since the item's life span will only decline with time, and the interest rates are typically high, no benefit is derived from purchasing these things with debt. A great number of such purchases rapidly decline in value, even after one use.

A significant benefit to good debts lies in the increase in cash flow that they commonly create. Properly structured good debts lead to tax advantages, to the ability to invest in still more assets that can produce cash, and to higher credit scores as well. Good debts that are paid on time furthermore build up a good financial base for the future. Good debts create cash flow, which stands in contrast to bad debts that do not.

Investments that produce passive income are among the best good debts. For example, purchasing an apartment building using debt will result in both income revenue and substantial tax deductions. This proves to be good debt, since although you are borrowing money, you are receiving passive income and gaining the ability to depreciate assets that can actually appreciate with time. On top of this, you are allowed to live there while you accrue all of these other benefits.

When considering a good debt, you should make certain that the income that the investment will provide is high enough to make the investment and the accompanying debt worth while. A number of experts offer advice on this. They suggest that not tying up in excess of twenty percent of your overall value in debt is a better practice. Higher debt levels than this can sound off warning bells with banks and other lenders.

Government National Mortgage Association (GNMA)

GNMA refers to a United States HUD Department of Housing and Urban Development based government corporation. This agency is different from its cousin Freddie Mac as Ginnie Mae is not a private corporation. Rather it is an actual U.S. government agency.

The roles of GNMA are two-fold. They are to guarantee there is sufficient liquidity for mortgages which are government insured. This comprises all mortgages provided by the FHA Federal Housing Administration, the RHA Rural Housing Administration, and the VA Veterans Administration. The other responsibility of Ginnie Mae is to attract the capital of investors into the marketplace for such loans. This allows for the various issuers to provide still more loans in the future. The majority of those mortgages which Ginnie Mae securitizes and sells are in fact MBS mortgage-backed securities which are guaranteed by the FHA. These are usually mortgages which are offered to lower income borrowers and first time home buyers.

GNMA operates in a fairly straightforward manner. The governmental agency purchases home mortgages off of the financial institutions which make such loans. Then it pools them together into $1 million and higher collections. Ginnie Mae has choices at this point. Some of these pools it holds on to and then directly sells them to investors outright. Others it sells off to financial institutions and mortgage bankers who then sell them on to investors themselves.

After this, either the mortgage banker or GNMA itself will collect mortgage payments off of the pools' mortgage homeowners. For those investors who choose to invest in a GNMA, they typically receive monthly payments which come with at least a portion of the principal (that remains outstanding) as well as an interest payment. The other method has investors just obtaining interest payments. In this case, the principal only comes back to the investors as the mortgage reaches maturity.

Sometimes investors call such bonds from the agency Ginnie Mae pass through securities. This is because the requisite mortgage payments will go through, or pass through, a bank. The bank then collects its fee in advance of passing on what remains of the payment to the appropriate investors. These payments amount to greater returns than comparable U.S. Treasury notes provide investors.

GNMA's also possess other advantages. They are guaranteed not to default and fail by the United States' government and its full faith and credit. They also prove to be extremely liquid. This is partly because they may be easily resold via the active secondary market at any time.

GNMA instruments come with a hefty minimum investment dollar requirement. This amounts to typically $25,000. Once this minimum threshold is met, the size may be increased in only single dollar increments to whatever level is desired. There are opportunities to purchase such Ginnie Mae's which can sell for under the standard $25,000 when they are occasionally offered at face value discounts via the secondary market. This could occur in cases where the applicable interest rates prove to be lower than more current instrument issues' rates or also as the remaining principals have become reduced significantly.

There are also mutual funds which buy into Ginnie Mae's. The cost of shares in such funds are considerably lower than the $25,000 minimum of the instruments themselves. In cases like this, investment trusts or outright Ginnie Mae funds will purchase the bonds directly from the government agency or secondary market. They will then provide their own shares, which represent stakes in such instruments, to the investing public.

It is not only separate investors who purchase the Ginnie Mae's. A great range of different organizations and companies purchase them. Several examples of these other buyers abound. They are credit unions, retirement pension funds, commercial banks, real estate investment trusts, corporations, and insurance companies. There are also a great variety of different institution kinds that actually issue such Ginnie Mae's. Among these are banks, mortgage companies, and credit unions.

Government Sponsored Enterprise (GSE)

A government sponsored enterprise is a financial service operations that the U.S. Congress created by law. Their purpose is to improve the amount of credit that flows into specific areas of the American economy. They were also intended to help those parts of the capital markets become more transparent and efficient as well as to lessen risks for investors and capital suppliers.

The wish of Congress in establishing them was to increase the available finance and lower the cost of obtaining it for certain specific segments of the economy. This was to be accomplished by encouraging investors via lowering the risks of losses to those involved.

The main components of the economy where these were set up were home finance, agriculture, and education. Among these, two of the government sponsored enterprises are best known. These are Fannie Mae, the Federal National Mortgage Association and Freddie Mac, the Federal Home Loan Mortgage Corporation.

The year 1916 saw the first government sponsored enterprise that Congress established. This was the Farm Credit System. Congress moved GSEs into housing finance in 1932 when it established the Federal Home Loan Banks. It focused on education costs and finance when in 1972 Congress chartered Sallie Mae. In 1995, Congress passed a law and permitted this educational GSE to give up its government sponsorship so that it could transform into a fully private company.

The segment of the economy for residential mortgages and borrowing proves to be substantially the largest industry where the government sponsored enterprises function. In mortgages, these GSEs own or pool around $5 trillion in home mortgages.

The way that Congress came up with to boost capital market efficiency and get past the imperfections of the market was to help funds migrate more effortlessly from fund suppliers to fund borrowers in major loan demand areas of the economy. They accomplished this with a type of government guarantee which limited the loss risks for those who offered the funds.

These government sponsored enterprises now mostly serve as intermediaries between agricultural and home borrowers and lenders. Freddie Mac and Fannie Mae remain the two best known and most influential GSEs today. They buy up mortgages and issue them through affiliated companies. Once this is accomplished, they pack them up as MBS mortgage backed securities. These securities come with the important financial backing from Freddie Mac or Fannie Mae. Investors allowed to trade in the TBA to be announced markets find these investments appealing when they carry government sponsored enterprises backing.

These housing GSEs also established a secondary market for loans with their guarantees, securitizing, and bonding. It has helped the main issuers of primary market mortgages to boost their volume of loans at the same time as they reduce the risks of single loans. It also gives investors a wide market of instruments which are securitized and standardized.

The government sponsored enterprise does not actually come with the government's hard guarantee of their credit. Despite this, lenders have always given them better interest rates at the same time that investors in the securities have paid high prices. This stems from the government's implicit guarantee that these critical organizations will not default or fail. It has helped the two main GSEs to save on borrowing costs to the tune of around $2 billion each year.

The subprime mortgage crisis and financial crisis reached a fevered pitch and embroiled Freddie Mac and Fannie Mae in 2007 and 2008. The American government demonstrated the value of the implicit guarantee then by bailing out and putting the two GSEs into conservatorship in September of 2008.

Graduated Payment Mortgage (GPM)

A graduated payment mortgage is a special type of home mortgage where payments are low initially and go up over the term of the loan. These are still considered to be a type of fixed rate mortgages as the interest rates are set and pre-determined even when the payments rise.

The low upfront payment helps financial institutions to qualify the borrowers. Banks only have to take into account the original low rate to approve them. This is why the GPMs assist those who otherwise would not be able to get qualified using the normal FRM fixed rate mortgage. This aids a great number of potential home buyers who might not be able to get qualified to purchase a home. It is best for younger or newer homeowners. Their levels of income should rise with time. This helps them to make the increasing mortgage payments.

The payments rise every year with a graduated payment mortgage until the entire amount has been repaid. The amount that they increase varies from one contract to the next. Typically the payments rises between 7% and 12% each year from the original base amount.

There is a danger with these types of products. If the young home buyers do not see their income rise consistently and significantly enough, the increasing payments on the home will take a greater share of their take home pay every year. Eventually, they may not be able to afford the payments if their salaries do not rise sufficiently.

The original payment for these graduated payment mortgages is not enough to cover the loan's interest. The difference between what is covered and what is not is called negative amortization. This amount adds on to the loan balance with every payment. It takes years for the rising payments to overcome this increase in the loan balance. Lenders do not like the fact that the balance goes up above the initial amount. Because of this they charge greater rates for these types of loans than they do for standard fixed rate mortgages.

The trade-off with a graduated payment mortgage is the larger payment that continues to grow for several years. This generally does not reach its peak level until five years have passed. The higher payment will then stay fixed for the rest of the mortgage term. This is the price to pay for a low upfront payment that a borrower can be approved for and can afford.

There are other kinds of graduated payment mortgages on the market. These alternatives provide varying rates of payment rises for different amounts of time. In one example, homeowners can get a gradually rising rate of 3% per year for ten years rather than pay more than 7% each year for 5 years. These alternative GPMs require a higher upfront payment amount and can also lead to a larger final payment. Because the initial payment is higher, the negative amortization will be less. This will cause the peak loan balance to be smaller.

GPMs are not unique in mortgages that have payments which increase. There are also fixed rate mortgages called temporary buy downs. These come with lower upfront payments during the loan's early years. The advantage to these is that the loan does not incur negative amortization.

Temporary buy downs only work if someone pays for the buy down account. The financial institution takes money from this supplemental account to cover the lower payments in the first two years. This way the lender receives identical payments for the entire life of the loan. Either the home seller or the buyer has to supply the money for the supplemental account.

HARP Program

HARP stands for the Home Affordable Refinance Program. This program that the government sponsored entities Fannie Mae and Freddie Mac created and back is unique. It turns out to be the one refinancing program that works with borrowers who are eligible and who have no or little equity in their houses so that they can receive refinancing benefits and lower interest rates.

The HARP program has changed some over the years. One of the main improvements to the program was to get rid of the underwater limitation amount for home owners. There is now no restriction on how much more the borrowers owe on their mortgage than the property is actually worth.

Thanks to this modification in the HARP program, a great number of home owners who could not qualify before will now be able to do so. The program itself expires on September 30, 2017. This makes it important for buyers who are considering it to take action on it or get more information in the near future.

The HARP program is a good choice for those borrower who have maintained a successful payment history over the last 12 months. It does not require a perfect payment record. Over the last six months there can not be any late payments. From six to twelve months prior there can only be a single payment that is 30 days late. The loan must also be guaranteed by or owned by Freddie Mac or Fannie Mae.

In order to participate, there are several other considerations. The loan only can be modified with this HARP program if it is either the primary residence or a second house or investment property. It makes most sense if the value on the house has declined. It is especially useful for those whose first mortgage amount is greater than the present house market value or if there is little equity in the property. The loan will only qualify if borrowers closed on them before or on May 31, 2009. This information can be obtained with the loan lookup tool and results on the Fannie Mae or Freddie Mac websites.

There are a number of good reasons for borrowers who are not able to take advantage of other refinancing means to utilize the HARP program on their mortgage. It lowers the monthly payment after the process is complete. The refinance procedure also decreases the interest rate. This means that borrowers will save on interest as well as monthly payment amounts.

It can be especially beneficial for those who have adjustable rate mortgages. These HARP interest rates are fixed, which means they will not change with time. Lower interest rates and less interest also help the home owners to build up their equity faster. It is possible to get a refinanced mortgage with a shorter term as well. Because the program does not require any appraisals, this saves the home owners both money and time that it takes to find someone to perform them to most banks' satisfaction.

Participating in the HARP program is not difficult. It requires that borrowers undergo an application process, receive approval, and finalize closing much like with the original mortgage. HARP lenders work with the home owners every step of the way and assist in deciding if the program meets the needs of the borrower. There may be closing costs associated with the refinance. These often can be rolled over into the new loan to reduce out of pocket costs as necessary.

Home Affordable Modification Program (HAMP)

The Home Affordable Modification Program is also known by its acronym HAMP. This stands for a program created by the United States government. They founded it in order to assist those homeowners who were struggling to keep up with their mortgages. For any homeowners who have watched in dismay as their financial conditions deteriorated since they originally purchased their house, they could be able to qualify for loan modifications to make keeping the home possible and affordable.

The program actually helps participants by allowing them to reduce their monthly mortgage payments. This happens as the program approves a lower rate of interest, extends the mortgage's time frame (and term), or alters the type of mortgage to fixed rate from adjustable rate ARM. In some cases, two or even three of these changes may be approved together. The modifications can happen because the United States government backs them.

The Home Affordable Modification Program began as the Departments of Housing and Urban Development HUD combined forces with the Treasury in order to forge a new initiative that they named Making Homes Affordable. Though there were other parts to this ground breaking concept, the HAMP proved to be a key pillar of it. The government recognized in the wake of the Great Recession that many Americans were only one accident, job loss, or illness away from falling hopelessly behind on their mortgages and payments. This is why they decided to come up with their innovative program for modifying mortgages to make them more affordable for those who are in the most need of help.

Becoming eligible for this home modification assistance program requires an applicant be able to successfully meet a particular set of criteria. They must have bought and financed the house before or on January 1st of 2009. They have to be capable of proving a real financial hardship that makes them struggle to meet their monthly mortgage payments. At the same time, they have to show that they are already behind on the monthly payments or even at risk of sliding into foreclosure of their home. In order to successfully qualify, the property can not have been condemned. They may not owe more than $729,750 on the primary residence which is a single family home. Finally, applicants may not show any personal real estate fraud convictions from any time within the past ten years.

If they meet all of these exacting criteria, then interested parties are able to call their specific mortgage servicer to inquire about any additional requirements that could exist with their particular company. It is also important to inquire if the mortgage servicing company even participates with the Home Affordable Modification Program in the first place. If the provider does participate and the applicant actually meets all of the minimum requirements for participation, then the home owner will need to speak with his or her lender in order to obtain all of the necessary paperwork and forms to enroll.

These forms include first the Request for Mortgage Assistance Form, or RMA. There is also the Income Verification Form as well as the IRS' 4605T-EZ form to complete. It is important to note that the final application does not get submitted to the government, but instead to the mortgage servicer. They will require a tangible proof of financial hardship when the individual submits this application.

There are actually a number of key benefits which this Home Affordable Modification Program delivers for successful applicants. They are able to sidestep foreclosure of the home, reduce their costs for keeping the house, obtain a new start on the mortgage, and better their credit history and rating. The home loan will be made to work for the owners so that they can simply modify the mortgage instead of losing the house.

Though the program is one that has helped a number of Americans, it is not the foolproof answer to irresponsible home buying and borrowing. There have been a number of homeowners who availed themselves of the program in HAMP only to re-default a second time. Some of these have actually forfeited their homes in the foreclosure process. The program has been shown in a recently conducted study that it can help a number of the fully 20 percent of homeowners who are not saving money which they might be able to by taking advantage of either a loan modification program such as this one or through refinancing their home.

Home Equity

Home Equity refers to those assets which result from the home owner's stake in the house itself. Calculating up the equity of the home is not difficult. One simply takes any remaining loan balances and subtracts them off of the market value of the property. It is very possible for the equity in a home to grow with time, in particular when the value of the property rises and also as the balance of the loan becomes gradually paid down over time.

An easier way to think of this home equity is as the part of the property which the home owner actually owns. The lender is always the interest holder in a given property that includes a mortgage secured by the home. This is the case all the way up to the point where the home owner pays off completely the mortgage loan balance. It is no exaggeration to state that the equity in a home is commonly the most valuable asset for most home buyers. Equity in a home allows for a home owner to take out a second mortgage at later points in the life of the mortgage loan.

It is always helpful to look at a real-world example to better understand difficult and challenging concepts such as this one. If a home buyer obtained a house for $250,000 and dutifully made a full 20 percent down payment, then he would likely obtain a $200,000 mortgage loan to pay the remaining balance on the house. The home equity at this initial point would equate to the down payment of $50,000. The home's value is $250,000, but the buyer only contributed $50,000 as an upfront down payment towards the purchase price.

In the unlikely event that the value of the home doubled, it would then be worth $500,000. Yet despite this windfall increase in value, the mortgage is still only $200,000. This would mean that the home equity increased to a massive $300,000. The equity stake then would have risen to 60 percent. Figuring this up is simply a function of dividing the balance of the loan by the market value to subtract the end result from one. Then the person must convert the resulting decimal into a percentage. While the balance on the mortgage has not grown, the equity in the home has massively increased.

There are several ways that a home owner might increase the equity within his home. The simplest way is to pay down the loan balance at a faster rate than only the monthly mortgage payment amounts. Slowly over time, these monthly payments will go more and more towards the principal repayment. It means that all else being equal, a person builds up the equity in the home at a rate that increases gradually every year. By making extra payments each month, which all accrue against the principal only, this equity grows faster and eventually exponentially so.

Another way equity accrues to a home is through home price appreciation. As the home grows in value (thanks to natural area appreciation or home improvement projects) the equity in the property similarly grows. Equity is always a handy asset, which makes it an integral part of the person's aggregate net worth. In an emergency or on a rainy day, home owners can simply withdraw large lump sum amounts from the equity of the house one day. This wealth might also be simply passed along down the family line to the owners' heirs as well.

There are two principle ways to withdraw the equity value from a house. It might be taken as a home equity loan or a home equity line of credit (called a HELOC). Either one will allow an individual to utilize the proceeds for practically anything they wish. This might be for home improvements, vacations, retirement, or university level education as a few examples.

Home Equity Line of Credit (HELOC)

A home equity line of credit is also known by its acronym HELOC. It represents a viable alternative to the more commonly used home equity loan. Whereas home equity loans provide lump sum amounts, Home Equity Lines of Credit provide cash as and when the borrower needs it. The downside to a HELOC is that a bank can decide to reduce the amount of available credit or cancel the line altogether without warning. This can happen before a borrower has utilized the funds.

In a home equity line of credit, borrowers use the equity within the home to be their collateral with the bank. The lending institution decides on the maximum amount that the borrower can obtain. The home owner then determines how much of this they want to borrow for the amount of time the bank permits. This might be until the monthly payments reduce the line to a zero balance, or it could be for a certain number of months. This makes these HELOCs much like a credit card in the ability to draw on the resources only when and as they need them.

The main difference between a home equity line of credit and a home loan is that the former is a revolving loan instrument. Borrowers are able to use the money then pay it off. They can then draw on it once again. Home equity loans pay a single lump sum up front amount one time. HELOCs also feature variable interest rates that will change over time, while home equity loans come with interest rates that are fixed. The payment amounts on the home equity loans are also fixed every month, while the payment on the HELOC depends on how much of the line is used.

In order to be able to obtain a home equity line of credit, the home owner must have significant equity in the house itself. Banks will insist that owners keep at least 10% to 20% equity within the property all the time. This must be the case after the line is approved as well. The HELOC approval process will also require verifiable proof of income, consistent documented employment, and a high credit score that is generally more than 680.

It is important for prospective borrowers to determine what they will use the home equity line of credit money for before they draw on it. Home renovations lend themselves better to home equity loans. This is because the one time large amount would enable the borrower to finish the renovations and then repay the loan. A HELOC is a better fit for a revolving bill such as the children's college tuition. Borrowers can use them to cover the tuition, then pay them off hopefully before the next tuition payment become due. At this point they can re-utilize the HELOC for the next semester tuition.

The home equity line of credit can also be a good choice for individuals who wish to consolidate the balances on their credit cards which feature high interest rates. The rates for the HELOC are typically much lower. This strategy requires some discipline. Once the credit cards have been cleared, there is the danger that the home owner might be tempted to run them back up again while they are still making payments on the line of credit. This would put borrowers in a worse situation than before they chose to consolidate.

Home equity lines of credit can get a home owner into the bad habit of constantly borrowing and paying them back as with a credit card. This can be a problem if the borrowers take on more debt with the HELOC than they can afford to pay in monthly payments. Missing these payments would put their home at jeopardy of being seized by the bank.

Home Equity Loan

A home equity loan is a means for home owners to borrow money using the value of their house. Borrowers find these loans appealing because they can usually borrow significant sums of money. Besides this, they are much simpler to get approved for than with many competing kinds of loans. A home owner's house secures these home equity loans. The borrowers may utilize these funds for any purpose that they wish. They do not have to be spent on expenses related to the house that secures the loan.

Such a home equity loan is actually a kind of second mortgage on a house. The first mortgage allows the buyer to purchase the home. When sufficient equity is established in the house, owners can attach other loans to the property to borrow against it.

There are a number of benefits to obtaining a home equity loan. They appeal to both lenders and borrowers. Borrowers get better APRs or interest rates from them than with other loan types. Because they are secured by the value of the home, they can be easier to get approved for even with bad credit. The IRS allows home owners to deduct interest expenses from these home equity loans from their taxes. Finally, borrowers are able to obtain substantial loan amounts using these loan vehicles.

The lenders like these loans because they consider them to be safer loans. The house acts as collateral in the process. This means that banks are able to seize the house to liquidate it and regain unpaid balances if the owner fails to make the payments. Because of this, banks know that borrowers will make the payments of these loans a high priority so they do not lose their house.

Banks protect themselves in any case by not lending too much against the value of the property. In general, lenders will not allow borrowers to obtain a greater amount than 85% of the value of the house. This includes both the amount that remains on the first mortgage as well as the second mortgage home equity loan. This percentage is known as the loan to value ratio. It can vary somewhat from one bank to the next.

The way home equity loans work is relatively straightforward. Borrowers receive a one time cash payment. They then make fixed payments each month to pay back the loan over a pre-set amount of time. The interest rate will be set by the bank at the beginning of the loan. With every payment, the loan balance declines after part of the interest costs are covered. This makes these amortizing loans.

Sometimes borrowers do not require all of the money at one time. An alternative to the home equity loan in this case is the HELOC home equity line of credit. This delivers a set amount of money which home owners can draw on only when and if they require it. The borrowers only have to pay interest on money which they physically draw and borrow. It is possible for the interest rate to change on these HELOC loans. Banks may also cancel such a line of credit before the borrower has utilized all or part of the funds.

Home equity loans can be used for many different needs. It is wise to improve the value of the house with the money through renovating, remodeling, or increasing the appeal of the property. Other common uses borrowers employ them for are to help pay for a second home, to afford college tuition and expenses for family members, or to consolidate bills with high interest rates.

HSBC

HSBC stands for Hong Kong Shanghai Banking Corporation. This largest international bank in the world by balance sheet has over $1.63 trillion in total assets. The British London based banking giant counts more than 47 million customers as part of its international network spanning 71 countries and territories and 6,000 offices around the globe.

HSBC was founded by a British businessman in 1865 to finance the growing trade between the West and Asia, and especially China. Today HSBC remains among the largest and most impressive banking and financial services conglomerate groups in the world by any relevant measure. Their stated goal is to be recognized as the globe's foremost and best respected international bank.

HSBC is operated globally through four major divisions. These include its Commercial Banking, Global Banking and Markets, Private Banking, and Retail Banking and Wealth Management divisions. Among the banking group's many achievements over the centuries, the group was responsible for setting up the modern day Chinese currency and banking system back during the reign of the last Chinese imperial dynasty. This financial and currency system which HSBC established for China is still used today.

HSBC Commercial Banking operates throughout 55 different nations and territories. Their operation covers both developing and developed world markets that are most important to their many customers. The division serves a great variety of customer types, ranging from major multinational corporations to small outfits to medium sized companies. It offers them the financial tools they need to run their operations effectively.

One of the bank's most appealing features is that it can call upon its vast and multinational financial strength to support clients with term loans, project and acquisition finance, and daily working capital. The bank also offers its customers the financial and legal know how to assist them in engaging in effective stock and bond issues and offerings.

The commercial banking group supports specialist staff in four primary fields. Global Liquidity and Cash Management provides businesses with tools to effectively manage their liquidity. The online platform helps the customers to transact payments seamlessly between currencies and countries. Global Trade and Receivable Finance offers financing to suppliers and buyers in the trade cycle so that they can cover their supply chains.

Global Banking offers its commercial customers a variety of services such as capital financing via equity, debt, and advisory services. Insurance and Investments provides protection in the form of financial, business, and trade insurance. It also offers wealth management for corporations, employee benefits, and other commercial insurance products to protect against risk.

The Global Banking and Markets division works with customers to help them access commercial opportunities for developed and developing markets. This division operates in three groups including the corporate sector group, the resources and energy group, and the financial institutions group. Services and products are comprised of financing, advisory, research and analysis, prime services, trading and sales, securities services, and transaction banking.

HSBC Private Bank delivers global private banking services that include wealth management, investment, and private banking services to its individual, business, and executive clients. The division's goal is to become the world's foremost private bank for business owners who are high net worth individuals leveraging the group's longstanding globally leading commercial services and heritage.

Retail Banking and Wealth Management provides its tens of millions of customers with a broad range of products and services. These include personal banking, internet banking, loans, mortgages, savings, insurance, investments, and credit cards. They offer a variety of proprietary services and accounts that include HSBC Premier, HSBC Advance, personal online banking, financial planning, and wealth solutions.

Interest Rate

Interest rates are the levels at which interest is charged a borrower for using money that they obtain in the form of a loan from a bank or other lender. These are also the rates that individuals and businesses are paid for depositing their funds with a bank. Interest rates are central to the running of capitalist economies. They are commonly written out as percentage rates for a given time frame, most commonly per year.

As an example, a small business might require capital to purchase new assets for the company. To acquire these, they borrow money form a bank. In exchange for making them this loan, the bank is paid interest at a pre set and agreed upon rate of interest for lending it to the company and putting off their own use of the monies. They receive this interest in monthly payments along with repayments of the principal.

Interest rates are also used by government agencies in pursuing monetary policies. Central banks set them to influence their nation's economic performance. They impact many elements of an economy such as unemployment, inflation, and investment levels.

There are several different interest rates to consider. The most commonly expressed one is the nominal interest rate. This nominal interest rate proves to be the amount of interest that is payable in money terms. If a family deposits $1,000 in a bank for a year, and is paid $50 in interest, then their balance by the conclusion of the year will be $1,050. This would translate to a nominal interest rate amounting to five percent per year.

The real interest rate is another type of rate used to determine how much purchasing power is received. It is the interest rate after the level of inflation is subtracted. Determining the real interest rate is a matter of calculating the nominal rate and removing the amount of inflation from it. In the example above, supposed the economy's inflation level is measured at five percent for the year. This would mean that the $1,050 in the account at year end only buys what it did as $1,000 at the beginning of the year. This translates to a real interest rate of zero.

Interest rates change for many reasons. They are altered for political gains of parties in power. By reducing the interest rate, an economy gains a short term boost. The help to the economy will often influence the outcome of elections. Unfortunately, the short term advantage gained is often offset later by inflation. This reason for changing interest rates is eliminated with independent central banks.

Another main reason that interest rates change is because of expectations of inflation. Since the majority of economies demonstrate inflation, fixed amounts of money will purchase fewer goods a year from now than they will today. Lenders expect to be compensated for this. Central banks raise interest rates to fight this inflation as necessary.

Interim Financing

Interim financing is a way of obtaining funding on a short term basis for a project. It can also be called gap financing or bridge financing. People or companies elects for this kind of financing for a specific purpose.

They may be seeking to get funding so that a project can be finished and start creating revenues. This would keep them from having to take resources away from other projects. This concept generally refers to loans. There are also cases of interim financing where companies utilize grants or other types of financial assistance.

A short term loan proves to be among the most frequently employed types of interim financing. These kinds of loans can be crafted so that the borrower will pay back the entire principle of the loan along with all of its interest in twelve months or less from the loan issue date.

This is the opposite of long term financing. In the longer term variety, the borrower receives several years to repay the loan. Loan deals on gap financing often come with interest rates that are a little higher than with longer term loans. For individuals or companies with excellent credit, financing companies can often offer extremely competitive interest rates on these short term loans.

A common use of interim financing is with construction projects that need to be finished. On an individual level, a consumer may wish to renovate either a room in the house or the entire home. The borrower may decide to obtain a short term loan at a better interest rate to cover the costs of labor and materials at the beginning of the project. This can save the borrower on the more substantial interest rates and fees for using credit cards or store credit with the various vendors. The end result is that the consumer spends significantly less money on the improvement project than he or she would by not utilizing the interim financing.

Real estate deals are another common use for this interim financing. A home owner may wish to move forward and buy a new house. The owner may need their present house to sell first. Short term loans like these can prove to be an optimal answer to the problem. Using the bridge loan the owner buys the house. The borrower can then repay the loan once their original house sells. This kind of strategy will help to push through the sale of the original house as well. The previous owners have already moved, which means the new owners can occupy the property without delay.

The goal of interim financing is to offer a short term bridge loan for the individual or business concerned. Despite this, sometimes a situation develops where the borrower will not be able to repay the loan as quickly as hoped. In this case, longer term or additional financing becomes necessary. Many lenders will work with the borrower in such a case to come up with a longer term financing program.

This will completely pay off the short term original loan. Additional money will usually be provided so that the borrower has the funds necessary to complete the project. This is especially the case with construction companies. It works out better for the borrower to engage in a rollover longer term loan than to take out another short term loan. The reason for this is that the longer term loans' finance rates are nearly always lower than the most competitive rates lenders will offer borrowers for short term bridge loans.

Investment Value

Investment Value refers to an asset's specific value given a particular range of investment parameters. It can be defined as the property value to a given group of investors (or an individual investor) who have specific investment goals in mind. This makes it a subjective measurement of the asset or property's value.

Many times potential investors will employ the investment value metric when they have an interest in buying a certain real estate property with a particular group of investment goals and objectives. It might be they have a targeted return rate they are looking for in the investment. This is why such a value metric heavily involves motivations and beliefs in a particular investment strategy.

The reason that this investment value would have importance on a transaction concerns buyers contemplating buying a given asset when they want to compare the pricing of the real estate or asset in question to the anticipated rate of return. When they are able to use this value to consider their specific rate of return, they are able to measure up the investment final results with the projected price they will pay out for the property. This helps them to make an intelligent purchasing decision consistent with their investment objectives.

In contrast to the investment value, market value is the true value of the property (or asset) in question based on the supply and demand of the open market. It is typically determined by utilizing the appraisal process where Real Estate is concerned. This contrasts with the individual investors' value they may place on the property as it pertains to their unique goals, objectives, and needs for the property they are considering.

It is important to realize that investment value is not the same as market value in many cases. The investment values might be lower, higher, or the same to the market values. This would heavily depend on the property's specific scenario at the time. In fact the market values and investing values are typically approximately the same. Yet they can diverge.

For example, investment value might be greater than that of the market value. A certain buyer may place a higher value on the property than would a typical informed purchaser. This could happen in the real world when a firm decides to expand its premises into a larger newer building that has just gone on sale across the road from the current company offices. The company might be willing to pay a higher price than the market value so that it could ensure competitors stay out of the market and do not secure the building before they can conclude the transaction. In such a scenario, this extra value becomes derived from the strategic advantage that the firm will realize by having the property.

Where a single investor is concerned, it is also possible for investment value to exceed the market value. An example of this could be when the investors have a special tax status or situation that can not be transferred. They might also have some type of highly advantageous financing terms that do not apply to rival investors or buyers.

It is similarly possible for investment value to be under that of the market value on a property. This could happen when the given property is not a kind in which the investors normally specialize or concentrate their efforts. As an example, for multifamily developers, choosing to consider developing a hotel could cause the investment value for this particular situation to be lower than the traditional market value for the given site. This would be because of the greater costs involved in learning to develop the property. It might also be that the investors are seeking out and demand a higher than average return from a property thanks to their current portfolio diversification and allocation.

Jumbo Loan

Jumbo loans are specific types of loans made by banks for home mortgages. They are special because these loans are for larger sized house loans. In order for a loan to be qualified as a jumbo one, it must be larger than the conforming loan limits.

The government Federal Housing Finance Agency sets these conforming loan limits through regulation. They are the agency that oversees the mortgage buying government sponsored entities Freddie Mac and Fannie Mae. Both of these groups purchase mortgages from the traditional lenders like banks and credit unions.

For the majority of the United States, jumbo loan limits start at $417,000. There are several states and a few hundred counties that have different loan limit amounts. Some of these limits range as high as $625,000 for their loan limits in areas that are the most expensive property markets.

Counting Louisiana parishes, Alaska boroughs, and the District of Columbia like counties, the U.S. has 3,143 counties. This does not consider the Virgin Islands, Guam, or Puerto Rico. An overwhelming majority 2,916 of these counties have the traditional limit amount of $417,000 for jumbo loan minimums.

Another 115 counties have loan limits that are in between the typical $417,000 and $625,000 maximum. This would include higher than usual priced real estate markets but not the most expensive ones like Los Angeles. In Colorado Denver County is one such example with a jumbo loan minimum of $458,850. Another 108 counties contain higher jumbo loan limits that start at $625,500. Included in these are the most expensive housing markets. Among these are such pricey counties as those found in New York City, Los Angeles, and San Francisco.

Several states and their counties are allowed to have higher conforming loan limits than the maximum amounts set out by the government housing authority. This includes Hawaii, Alaska, the Virgin Islands, and Guam. These are all treated specially because of a long time exception to the regulation. In Hawaii for example, four of its five counties have the highest limits for jumbo loan cutoffs. They range from $657,800 to $721,050.

Obtaining a jumbo mortgage involves some extra paperwork and proofs. Underwriting for these jumbo types is much the same as with standard conforming mortgages. There are more requirements for appraisals and down payments than with smaller mortgages. Some jumbo mortgage lenders have a requirement for two appraisals rather than the standard single one.

Down payments are also often more demanding for jumbos than for the traditional mortgages. Usually these lenders will want a higher down payment to ensure the individual can really afford and is committed to the loan. The minimum down payments for these more expensive home purchases will vary with each lender. They might be as high as 30%, or they could be as low as 15% to 20%.

Only applicants with significant finances need apply for these jumbo loans. A great number of their lenders require a minimum high credit score of 700 or better. They also insist on a debt to income ratio that does not exceed 43%. These lenders will want to see minimally from six to twelve months' cash reserves in bank accounts as well.

Jumbo loans are not only made to individuals for their primary residences. Lenders will also issue them for vacation or second homes. Investment properties may also involve jumbo loans. They come with a wide range of terms and interest rates.

Jumbo loans can be issued as adjustable rate loans or fixed rate loans. They often come with higher interest rates than individuals would pay for conforming loans or for high balance conforming home loans. Sometimes in addition to the bigger down payment the underwriting standard will be stricter as well.

Lease

Leases are contracts made between an owner, or lessor, and a user, or lesee, covering the utilization of an asset. Leases can pertain to business or real estate. There are a variety of different types of leases that vary with the property in question being leased.

Tangible property and assets are leased under rental agreements. Intangible property leases are much like a license, only they have differing provisions. The utilization of a computer program or a cell phone service's radio frequency are two example of such an intangible lease.

A gross lease is another type of lease. In a gross lease, a tenant actually gives a certain defined dollar amount in rent. The landlord is then responsible for any and all property expenses that are routinely necessary in owning the asset. This includes everything from washing machines to lawnmowers.

You also encounter leases that are cancelable. Cancelable leases can be ended at the discretion of the end user or lessor. Other leases are non cancelable and may not be ended ahead of schedule. In daily conversation, a lease denotes a lease that can not be broken, while a rental agreement often can be canceled.

A lease contract typically lays out particular provisions concerning both rights and obligations of the lessor and the lessee. Otherwise, a local law code's provisions will apply. When the holder of the lease, also known as the tenant, pays the arranged fee to the owner of the property, the tenant gains exclusive use and possession of the property that is leased to the point that the owner and any other individuals may not utilize it without the tenant's specific invitation. By far the most typical type of hard property lease proves to be the residential types of rental agreements made between landlords and their tenants. This type of relationship that the two parties establish is also known as a tenancy. The tenant's right to possess the property is many times referred to as the leasehold interest. These leases may exist for pre arranged amounts of time, known as a lease term. In many cases though, they can be terminated in advance, although this does depend on the particular lease's terms and conditions.

Licenses are similar to leases, but not the same thing. The main difference between the two lies in the nature of the ongoing payments and termination. When keeping the property is only accomplished by making regular payments, and can not be terminated unless the money is not paid or some form of misconduct is discovered, then the agreement is a lease. One time uses of or entrances to property are licenses. The defining difference between the two proves to be that leases require routine payments in their term and come with a particular date of ending.

Lease-to-Own Purchase

A Lease-to-Own Purchase is a combination of a lease on a house with a purchase option on the home. This option is valid for a specific amount of time, typically for 3 years or less. The price for the purchase is agreed on in advance and is a part of the contract. These types of arrangements became far more common after the housing crisis and Great Recession. Many individuals who wanted to buy a house could no longer qualify for the stricter loan requirements. This also impacted sellers who could not obtain a selling price with which they were satisfied by any other means.

With a Lease-to-Own Purchase, the contract is typically designed and provided by the seller. The benefits of the arrangement can be set up to provide advantages to both buyer and seller parties. They might also be arranged so that the majority or even all of the benefits accrue to one side. This means that buyers should beware before entering such an agreement. It is wise for them to share the contract with a real estate attorney before they sign.

In a traditional Lease-to-Own Purchase contract, borrowers first pay an option fee that goes against the cost of buying the house. This generally amounts to from 1% to 5% of the home price. The renter will also pay a fair market value rent alongside a rent premium that also goes towards the price of buying the house. Everything is negotiable in these contracts, including option period, option fee, rent premium, rent, and the price of the house. Should the purchase option not be exercised by the renter, then he or she forfeits the rent premium and the option fee to the seller.

Buyers will naturally want a longer option period. This gives them a greater amount of time in which to repair their credit and save up money for a down payment. The downside to a longer option period in a Lease-to-Own Purchase comes into play if they can not exercise the option to buy. In this case, the renters forfeit both the option fee and the monthly rent premium which they have paid continuously. Sellers will want a shorter time period on the option. If they make it too short, they will be unable to sell the house to the renter.

It is possible for a Lease-to-Own Purchase to work out to be a win-win situation for both parties. The rent premium and option fee to the buyers represent equity they are paying into the house which they expect to buy. Such payments are compensation towards a guarantee for the seller that the house will sell. The seller will get to keep the additional payments as income if the buyer is unable to obtain the mortgage needed to purchase the property.

Some Lease-to-Own Purchase contracts will provide the renter with the ability to sell their option to another party. Such an option gives buyers additional confidence in the deal in the event that they are unable to personally exercise their buying option. This is a concession from sellers who would rather keep the house along with the fees they have collected. Some lease contracts will also have clauses that can cancel the buyer's option. These are often set as penalties for late rent payments.

One advantage to leasing the house before buying it lies in buyer awareness. The renters have time to consider any significant problems with the house, neighbors, or the neighborhood before they commit. If these are substantial issues, the buyers are able to cut their losses and not go through with the buying option.

Leasehold Estate

A Leasehold Estate relates to an official and legal interest that permits a company or individuals to assume temporary ownership of the land of another individual or company. They are able to use this land for business purposes, agricultural applications, or even as a dwelling. Property could include timber land, mineral land, oil land, farm land, or business and/or residence property. With such leasehold estates, landlords possess the title of the property at the same time as the tenant holds the rights to utilize said property. These estates range wildly in the format for the agreement and how it is set up, the amount of time the status exists, and the kind of property which is being leased.

A Leasehold Estate can be established orally or as a written agreement. Those agreements which are intended to endure over a year might have to be composed in a written document per the laws of the relevant state which has jurisdiction. These agreements provide either explicit or implicit permission for all the receiving end parties, who are called the lessees, to assume control of the said property of the other party, who is referred to as the lessor.

There are other various kinds of property agreements which exist. What separates leasehold agreements from these competing formats, such as purchase agreements, is the actual termination date. Every party which is involved with a leasehold agreement comprehends that the agreed upon ownership interests will eventually conclude. This is to say that they are not intended to last in perpetuity. Another distinctive feature of such estates lies with the lessee's right to possess the said property in question. Various other kinds of property agreements, like licenses or easements, actually provide the holder with the permanent rights to utilize the property as they see fit.

Leasehold Estates are quite specific. They comprise both land and any property on the land in question at a given address. Land in this sense of the word does not simply mean the physical land, but also includes any buildings which lie on the property. It also applies to any and all natural resources which occupy the land in question. These estates could also include other forms of personal property, like machinery or fixtures which are so permanently a part of the land that they become considered to be part and parcel of the property. Such fixtures could comprise things like fencing, lighting, wells, or windmills.

Estates are types of personal property. Applicable state laws commonly govern the legal definition of personal property. This means that they could supersede clauses within the Leasehold Estate agreement. An example of this is found in the state of California. The leasehold which pertains to agricultural purposes may not be extended past a maximum time frame of 51 years total.

This is why such leasehold agreements are established with a pre-determined and limited number of years in mind. This is articulated in the tenancy of years. Such a specified length of lease is determined by both lessor and lessee. The only exception is when state laws set the time span directly. It is possible to terminate such a leasehold tenancy ahead of the articulated time. The lessee must decide to surrender his or her possession of the property at the same time as the lessor agrees to resume control over his property and rights.

Four different classifications of these Leasehold Estates exist. They are fixed term, periodic, at will, and at sufferance. Fixed term tenancy refers to the number of years of the tenancy. It is states as an interest which is established to endure a particular amount of time.

Periodic tenancy relates to a set out amount of time, as with week to week, month to month, or even year to year. The leasehold can be ended by either tenant or landlord simply giving a notice to vacate the property. Usually a 30 days notice in writing must be provided to the owner of the property.

Tenancy at will refers to the lack of structure with these kinds of leasehold agreements. No date is given for the end of tenancy in such a form of leasehold estate. Tenancy at sufferance happens as a tenant decides to overstay the date of termination as spelled out in the applicable agreement. Landlords in these cases possess the legal rights to simply evict the tenant if they wish.

Lender

Lenders are individuals or more commonly institutions that loan out money. The person who receives this money is a borrower. A number of different kinds of lending organizations exist. These include commercial, mutual organizations, educational, hard money, and lenders of last resort.

Commercial lenders are the most common of the traditional lenders. Commercial types are usually banks. Another kind of commercial lender would be a private financial organization. Commercial lenders provide offers on their loans to their borrowers at a set rate of loan terms. Such terms include time frame of the loan and the interest rate. Their goal is to make as much money as possible relative to the chances of the borrower not repaying the loan.

Mutual organizations are another type of lender. They are composed of members of the mutual who cooperate together to loan money to the membership. The members pool their money into the organization. From there it is loaned out to the members who need to borrow money. They do this with favorable terms and at advantageous rates.

Mutual organizations are not driven to make profits. This allows them to offer lower interest rates on the loans they make and higher interest rates on the deposits they take. Among these mutual groups are community based credit unions. Friendly Societies are another example of them.

Educational lenders provide loans to individuals who are looking to further their education at an institution of higher learning like a college or university. They offer borrowers subsidized or unsubsidized loans. When the loans are subsidized, the Federal Government guarantees the loans and ensures that the lender provides a low and often fixed interest rate.

Hard money lenders make special types of loans that are short term. These are loans principally secured by real estate collateral. The downside to this kind of a lender is that they often provide higher interest rates than a traditional commercial bank. The tradeoff is that they will often take on a larger variety of deals.

Typically these hard money lenders give terms that are more flexible to their borrowers. Some states have stricter laws on interest rates that may be charged than does the Federal government. This forces hard money lenders to operate under different rules and with lower interest rates when they are in conflict with usury laws in give states.

Many times these loans that lenders make to individuals become brokered loans. In such cases, third parties consider the borrower's case then send the loan request out to a variety of lenders. This is often done over the Internet. They pick these different lenders because of their chance of approving the borrower in question. Sometimes the terms can be improved by one or more of these competing lenders in order to win over the borrower's business.

Lenders of last resort are an interesting final category. They are often governmental organizations whose goal is to save national economies and important banks from failure. These types of organizations loan money out to too big to fail banks which are close to collapse. They do this to safeguard the bank's depositors and to prevent panic from pushing the nation's economy into a downward spiral.

Lenders of last resort can also be private organizations that make loans to individuals. These groups loan out money to borrowers who present great risks of default or who have extremely low credit scores. Interest rates with these lenders are substantially higher than with traditional lenders. They charge these rates in order to make up for the losses they suffer from their borrower's greater default rates. Such lenders that charge even higher rates are sometimes known as loan sharks.

Lender of Last Resort

Lender of Last Resort refers to an official central financial institution which provides emergency loans to commercial and savings banks as well as other financial institutions which are suffering from extreme financial hardship or are believed to be nearing collapse. Generally such a lender turns out to be a national central bank. Within the U.S., it is the Federal Reserve which functions as the last case lender to those institutions which find themselves without any other way to borrow funds quickly. Their inability to gain access to funds and credit could lead to a devastating consequence for the greater economy in general. This is why the central banks will provide credit extensions on an expedited basis to those financial institutions which are undergoing extreme financial stress and so in consequence cannot get funds from anywhere else.

The principal job of such a Lender of Last Resort is to maintain the financial system stability and the banking system integrity through safeguarding the deposited funds of individuals and businesses. This is critical to foster confidence in the financial system and to prevent wholesale panic from taking hold of depositors who might otherwise cause runs on the banks by attempting to draw out all of their funds at once. Such an action would create an illiquidity event for the bank and force them to close their doors.

It has been over a century and a half since central banks made it their missions to head off great depressions through being the effective Lenders of Last Resort when financial crises erupted. The action does deliver the liquidity funds with a penalty interest rate. As open market operations take over the funding facility, the interest rate drops for safe assets as collateral. The process also includes direct support to the market.

Commercial banks do not enjoy borrowing from the Lender of Last Resort at any time. It would be a sure fire warning that the bank was undergoing financial stress or even experiencing a crisis of liquidity and a crisis of confidence would next follow. This is the reason that critics of this type of arrangement feel that it tempts banks into taking on a higher level of risk than they should in a form of moral hazard. This could happen because they believe that consequences for engaging in risky financial behavior will not be so severe.

The alternatives to a trustworthy central banking institution not functioning as a Lender of Last Resort can be serious. Bank runs are what result in times of financial crisis when the customers of banks begin to show concern over the solvency of their home financial institution. These customers can be seized with sudden panic and descend en masse on the bank demanding to withdraw all of their funds when confidence in the individual bank or the banking system as a whole erupts.

Banks only maintain s tiny percentage of their deposited funds on hand in their vaults. This is how a bank run can result in the liquidity of a bank rapidly disappearing. Literally these panicked customer actions can set into motion a self-fulfilling prophecy which leads to the bank failing as a result of insolvency.

This actually occurred in 1929 and throughout the 1930s. Bank runs led to catastrophic and widespread bank failure throughout the United States after the 1929 stock market crashes. This snowballed into the Great Depression which gripped the country and developed world economies for the next roughly fifteen years. The American federal government responded too late with tough new legislation which mandated severe reserve requirements on the banks. It required by law that they keep a specific minimum percentage of their deposits as available cash reserves.

Lien

A lien is a claim on one individual's property by another person or entity. The party that holds the lien is able to recover the property if a debtor will not follow through with making payments. There are also other circumstances in which liens would allow the lien holder to take the property. Mortgages on houses or buildings prove to be one kind these. Vehicle loans for a business or individual represent other types that are put on the value of the vehicle. When the obligation is paid off, the lien becomes discharged.

Before individuals are able to receive their money after the sale of an asset like a car or house, the lien must be paid off first. With a vehicle, this means that the lender will not send out the title until they receive complete repayment of the principal.

The majority of liens allow for the individuals or businesses to utilize the property as they are paying it. There are scenarios where the lender or creditor physically holds the property while the borrower is making payments. These are a part of bankruptcy procedures as well because they are secured loans with debt repayment rules that have to be addressed in a case.

While there are a number of different types of liens, the most typical one is on a vehicle. Individuals buy a car from the dealer. The bank loans the money and secures the loan. They do this by placing a vehicle lien which allows them to hold on to the automobile's title. The lender files a UCC-1 form to record this. So long as the debtor continues to make payments, the loan will be paid off finally. The bank would then release to the individual the title.

If the individuals stop making their payments, the bank is able to take possession of the vehicle back while still holding the title. If the vehicle owners choose to sell the automobile when they still owe principal, they must clear the bank loan in order to obtain the title. Without the title, a person can not sell the vehicle.

There are a variety of different types of liens in the world. Consensual ones are those which individuals voluntarily accept when they buy something. Non consensual ones are also known as statutory. These come from a court process where an entity places a lien on assets because bills have not been paid. Three of these are fairly common.

A tax lien occurs when individuals do not pay local, state, or federal income taxes. These are put on the offender's property. A judgment lien comes as a result of a case in a small claims court. When a court gives a judgment to one party, the offending party might refuse to pay. In this case the court will place a judgment lien on the offender's property.

A mechanic or contractor lien happens when a contractor performs a job for a home owner. If the owner refuses to pay, the contractor can ask a court to place a lien on the property in question. This would have to be paid off along with other security interests before the property owner is able to sell.

Loan Modification

A loan modification proves to be a set of changes on the original terms and conditions of a mortgage loan agreement. These must be agreed to by both the borrower and the lender. The housing crisis of 2007 caused many American homeowners to be on the verge of foreclosure. The numbers of imminent and in process foreclosures increased dramatically.

Loan modifications were amended to be a means for home owners to stay out of foreclosure and keep their houses. The process is not simple or quick, and it can be time consuming. Consumers also have to watch out for scams that prey on the vulnerable owners of homes.

Before the financial crisis erupted, a loan modification turned out to be a means for borrowers to ask for better interest rates on their mortgages without having to undergo an entire refinancing ordeal. Every mortgage company did not offer them. The ones that featured these would provide them for a cost to borrowers on the condition that their mortgage had not been resold to another firm. Now they are far more commonplace since lenders needed unorthodox solutions to help homeowners who were struggling to keep up with their payments and avoid foreclosure.

For the process of a loan modification to begin, the borrower must first request such a change to the loan terms. These changes once only affected the interest rate and made them lower. The more recent packages offered since the Great Recession are even able to change adjustable rate mortgages into standard fixed rate types. It is possible that a lender could suggest such a change to its borrowers as a possibility. Usually the borrowers initiate the process by determining they can not keep up with their loan payments and asking for help and a modification.

The next step is for the lender to consider the borrower's request. They are not required to agree to these petitions. A great number of lenders have very strict guidelines on which borrowers they will approve for modifications and which they will not. This is the case even when the homeowner has foreclosure looming. It is partly because such modification programs were not created to save home owners from rising adjustable interest rates or payments they could not handle. They were made to create a cheaper way of refinancing down to better interest rates. Each lender makes its own rules for which modifications they will accept and which they will reject.

Finally the lender will decide whether to approve or reject the modification request. They will then notify the borrower in writing. Many borrowers are rejected because they have been late with their mortgage payments frequently or too recently. Other lenders might not be in possession of the original loan any more. Whatever the reason is, the lender will state this in the letter.

If the request for modification gains approval, the request goes through to the department that handles loan servicing. There the loan will be modified to the new terms and conditions. Usually this will only reduce the interest rate and not change the loan's amortization. It may require several payment periods before these changes take effect. This is why borrowers should always keep making the payments in the amount and time for which they are scheduled.

Loan to Cost Ratio

Loan to Cost Ratio, or LTC, proves to be a measurement utilized by finance companies in extending loans for commercial real estate projects. It is employed ultimately to make comparisons of the offered financing for a given building project versus the expenses of completing said project. With the LTC ratio, lenders of commercial real estate loans are able to decide on the risks involved in backing a particular construction project via loans. The LTC ratio is similar to the LTV loan to value ratio. They both compare the amount of the construction loan to the value in fair market terms of the project in question.

Lenders work with the Loan to Cost Ratio in order to decide what loan percentage or dollar amount the financier is agreeable to finance. They do this with a basis on the firm costs stated in the construction project budget. After construction completes, these projects then possess a new and often times significantly higher value. Future values can often be double what the construction costs prove to be. This means that on a loan for $200,000 in construction, the future value of the project is likely to be $400,000 once it is fully concluded.

Consider how LTC will look in this example. With $200,000 in construction costs, and an 80% LTC ratio, the lender would be willing to loan out $160,000 on the total project. Using a similar 80% LTV ratio metric instead would significantly change the amount of money the lender is wiling to extend to $400,000 x 80% for $320,000.

Lenders never completely finance 100% of construction costs. This is because they feel that the builders also need to have significant exposure to the project in order to guarantee they will give their all to see them succeed. This is what is meant by the colloquial expression "skin in the game." It prevents a builder from simply getting up and walking away from a project gone bad. It is why the majority of lenders will require a builder to kick in minimally 10% to 20% of the construction costs to secure a financing deal.

Loan to value ratios are not the same as the Loan to Cost Ratio, though they have much in common up to a point. LTV evaluates the loan issued versus the project value once it will be fully completed. Since most banks assume that construction projects will double in value once they are finished, this is why an identical LTV percentage to the LTC ratio will yield twice the loan amount.

Lenders hold firmly to the LTC ratio. It helps them to clearly express the levels of risk in a given financing project for commercial construction. In the end, using a greater Loan to Cost Ratio will entail a significantly riskier project from the lender's perspective. This is why the overwhelming majority of reputable mainstream lenders will not surpass a pre-determined percentage when they consider any given project. They usually limit this amount strictly to a maximum of 80% of the project's LTV or LTC. When lenders are willing to become involved at a higher percentage and ratio, they will most always insist on a substantially greater project and loan interest rate to compensate them for the additional level of risk to which they are consenting.

Lenders will also have to consider other information and circumstances beyond simply Loan to Cost Ratio and Loan to value ratios when extending such financing. They take into consideration the value of the property and its location for where the project will be constructed. They also contemplate how much creditworthiness and experience the commercial builders in the application possess. Finally, they consult both the borrowers' loan payment histories on other loans and their credit record as demonstrated in their company credit report.

Loan-to-Value-Ratio (LTV)

The Loan to Value Ratio is commonly known by its acronym LTV. This loan to value ratio states the total value of the first mortgage against the full real estate property's appraised value. The formula for figuring this ratio is simply the amount of the loan divided by the property value. It is expressed as a percent. So if a borrower is seeking $180,000 with which to buy a $200,000 house, then the Loan to Value Ratio is ninety percent.

The loan to value ratio proves to be among the most critical risk factors that lenders consider when they are deciding whether to qualify borrowers for a mortgage loan on a house. The dangers of a default occurring most influence the loan officers in their lending decisions. The chances of an institution having to take a hit in a foreclosure procedure only goes up as the dollar amount of the property equity goes down. Because of this, as the Loan to Value ratio goes up, the qualification tests for many mortgage programs get significantly stricter. Some lenders will insist on a borrower who comes with a high loan to value ratio on the property in question to purchase mortgage insurance. This safe guards the lender from any default realized by the borrower, but it also raises the mortgage's total costs.

Property values used in the loan to value ratio are generally set by appraisers. Still, the most accurate value of a piece of real estate is undoubtedly that determined when a willing seller and willing buyer come together to agree on a sale. Usually, banks decide to go with the lower number when they are offered choices of a purchase price that is fairly recent or an appraisal value. Recent sales are commonly deemed to be those that happened from a year to two years ago, although every bank makes its own rules in this regard.

When a borrower selects a property that he or she will purchase with a lower loan to value ratio that is less than eighty percent, lower interest rates can many times be obtained by borrowers who are low risk. Higher risk borrowers will also be considered in such a scenario, meaning those who have prior histories of late payments on mortgages, who have lower credit scores, who have high loan requirements or higher debt to income ratios, and who have neither sufficient cash reserves nor requested income documentation. Generally, higher loan to value ratios are only permitted for those borrowers who have a reliable mortgage payment history and who possess greater credit scores. Only those buyers with the greatest credit worthiness are considered for one hundred percent financing that translates to a one hundred percent loan to value ratio.

Loans that are made to the standards of lending giants Freddie Mac and Fannie Mae and their guidelines can not have loan to value ratios that exceed or are equal to eighty percent. Any loans higher than this percentage of eighty percent must come with attached private mortgage insurance. The private mortgage insurance premiums simply go on top of the existing mortgage principal and interest payments.

Loss Mitigation Program

Loss Mitigation Program refers to a special vehicle which arose during the latter years of the global financial crisis and preceding subprime mortgage crisis. This happened because of the 2008 subprime mortgage crisis which the American economy suffered from at that time.

It started because of an enormous bursting of the housing prices bubble that caused a substantial rise in delinquencies and foreclosures of mortgages. Next a collapse in the value of all home-backed securities occurred, including in the now-infamous MBS mortgage backed securities.

The economy continued to struggle to recover even four years later in 2012. Banks had been bailed out of their poorly made loans by the United States Treasury and Federal Government. Homeowners received no real such help at first though. They had no recourse but to try to manage their higher interest rates at the same time as their home prices had declined substantially.

Fortunately for homeowners across the United States, one court intervened on behalf of consumers in the Western part of the state of Pennsylvania. It was this Bankruptcy Court for the Western District of Pennsylvania that took great initiative and developed the Loss Mitigation Program late in the year 2012. The program finally offered beaten down homeowners the ability to modify their mortgages in a court-overseen program which the banks administered directly.

This Loss Mitigation Program began in an effort to offer clarity on failing mortgages. The idea was to fast track the process of loan modification for both the lenders and the borrowers who were involved. It is true that many mortgage and finance companies had already developed their own internal programs for mortgage modification after the mortgage meltdown happened in 2008. Still the process for obtaining such a modification was overwhelming as homeowners dealt with tedious procedures and often saw little to no end results.

The Loss Mitigation Program became necessary because the HAMP Home Affordable Modification Program which the federal government had sponsored had not prevented defaults at what the Special Inspector General for the TARP called an "alarming rate." HAMP had been created originally to assist homeowners who needed to modify their government FHA insured mortgages, to stay out of foreclosure, and to lower their high monthly payments.

Yet according to this watchdog group, by the conclusion of March in 2013, more than 312,000 participants in the program had realized default on their mortgages. The U.S. Treasury could not come up with any one reason to explain why these default rates had grown so egregiously. Some participants in the program revealed that they only benefited from a modification which was temporary in the initial trial period of the mortgage modification program.

This is why the Loss Mitigation Program began. It was an effort to help the homeowners obtain real and lasting relief so that they could stay in their homes. The program worked according to a simple process which involved four steps. First homeowners had to file for bankruptcy protection in order to safeguard all of their assets and reduce or eliminate their other debts. This allowed them to concentrate their available income on keeping the residential property.

Next the homeowner would engage a bankruptcy attorney to file motions that enrolled the individual into this Loss Mitigation Program. In other words, the modification program existed beneath the umbrella of the bankruptcy protection. Third, the court would approve the application then sign an order that laid out strict procedural guidelines for both lender and borrowers. Clear deadlines were spelled out for both borrowers and lender. It ensured the process became instantly transparent for borrowers since the mortgage modification package and mortgage status had to be treated in good faith by the mortgage company.

Finally, the program set up an electronic portal through which all relevant correspondence on the process had to pass. The court's representatives would monitor the correspondence to be certain that the two parties were carrying out their responsibilities and roles in good faith.

Thanks to this portal, the Loss Mitigation Program process became streamlined, time saving, and cost reducing for all of the concerned parties.

The entire process had to be completed in 60 days unless either the lender or borrower sought out and explained a valid reason for requiring extra time. Serious consequences were mandated for either party delaying the process unnecessarily.

Loss to Lease

Loss to lease is a phrase that is used in real estate property leasing, particularly pertaining to apartment complexes or senior assisted living facilities. Loss to lease is also an accounting line in the books of rental properties and apartment complexes. In both cases, it refers to income on leases that is potentially lost through making incentive offers to prospective tenants whom you hope to lease a unit in a property.

Examples of loss to lease are helpful to understand the concept. Some apartments will offer one free month's rent with a six or twelve month lease contract. The amount of this lost month's rent would be the loss to lease figure for the leasing property and the leasing property's books. Other examples involve loss to lease figured up on a monthly basis. Should the potential revenue from rent amount to only $500 when the market rate for rental is $550, then the loss to lease comes out to be $50 per month.

Cash flow is the part of a rental property books where loss to lease most commonly appears. When required, it can be figured up using a simple formula. The scheduled base rental revenue is determined. This figure has the potential market rent subtracted from it to come up with the Loss to Lease result.

The interesting thing about loss to lease is that it has no meaningful impact on a rental property or apartment complex's cash flow bottom line. Instead, it only represents an accounting number. Loss to lease does not offer any advantages to a company or individual when they are figuring up and filing their taxes either, since it does not represent any actual real or tangible loss in income, only loss in potential income, or hoped for income.

Market Value

With regards to real estate, market value is the price which a real property seller can anticipate obtaining from the property purchaser in normal open and fair market negotiations. In general, appraisers value a home or other piece of real estate property utilizing a number of critical factors. When markets are volatile, such prices will vary significantly. Real estate agents may place one value on a home or other piece of real estate, yet in the end, the true property value is only what an able and willing buyer will actually pay to acquire it.

It is crucial to be aware of the market value of a piece of property individuals or businesses are selling as this ultimately sets the asking price of the real estate in question. Those sellers who are not intimately aware of this will either overprice their houses or under price them. Either of these actions will often lead to poor financial results. Not being aware of a property's true value can cause homeowners to become victims to practices of predatory lending. In this unscrupulous lending behavior, the bank or other lending financial institution will prevail upon a borrower to take out a greater amount of money than their property is really worth.

It is real estate agents or better still professional appraisers who determine most accurately the market value of a house or piece of real estate through measuring it up to other properties in the area or neighborhood which share similarities with the one in question. Real estate agents and appraisers call such recently sold area properties "comparables." They will always seek to find houses which are as alike in style, size, and location to the one they are appraising as possible.

Such properties must have sold within the prior six months to a year. According to this strategy, the professionals will similarly discern what the typical price per square foot of the houses in the area actually is. This practice by itself will not set the market price of a house, but it will give the professionals a good starting point from which to set a reasonable and viable asking price for the property.

There are also various other factors which influence a property's market value. These include the condition of the property in question as well as any improvements which the seller makes. Where a home is concerned, bathroom and kitchen renovations and updates are the main ones which will boost the selling price. Other more cosmetic appearance improvements like new carpet, fresh paint, updated light fixtures, and special window treatments will help a house to show better and perhaps sell faster, yet they will not increase the all around value of the home.

Yet it is absolutely true that the overall condition of any piece of real estate will impact its total value. Houses that boast more current and better maintained appliances and systems, roofs, windows, and even entry doors will realize a significantly better final selling price than those which offer flawed structures or outdated appliances, systems, entry doors, and mechanics.

In corporations and investments, market value is the price for which a given asset will sell in the open market. This measure of value can often be applied to the market capitalization of any company which is publically traded. Determining the market cap value is a matter of multiplying out the current price per share by the quantity of total outstanding shares.

This measure of market value is simplest to calculate for those instruments which are traded on exchanges, like futures and stocks. This is because their market prices are readily available and commonly disseminated. With over the counter securities such as fixed income securities, it can be far harder to ascertain. Yet the most difficult to determine market values are those commonly associated with less liquid assets such as businesses and real estate. This is why business valuation experts and real estate appraisers determine the market values for such assets as these.

MERS

MERS stands for the Mortgage Electronic Registration Systems. It is also a privately owned and operated company that maintains this electronic database and registry whose purpose is to follow the ownership of and servicing rights to American mortgage loans.

This MERS represents a revolutionary way of vastly simplifying the means of keeping track of how both mortgage servicing and ownership rights can be originated, sold, and followed. The Real Estate finance industry actually created it. MERS boasts that it does away with the requirement to create and record assignments as both commercial and residential loans are being exchanged.

The mortgage banking industry got together to come up with a way to simplify the process of working with mortgages through utilizing e-commerce to reduce and even eliminate paper. The mission of the company and its database lies in registering literally all mortgage loans within the U.S. on the MERS system.

MERS actually performs its role on behalf of the servicer and the lender in handling county land records. Loans that are registered on the MERS system can not have problems with future assignments since MERS is always the nominal mortgagee, regardless of the number of times that a mortgage servicing is sold. MERS is approved to be original mortgagee by all of the major lending outfits, including Freddie Mac, Fannie Mae, Ginnie Mae, the VA, the FHA, and both Utah and California Housing Finance Agencies, along with each of the Wall Street ratings agencies.

Many groups benefit from the existence of the MERS registry. This includes mortgage servicers, originators, wholesale lenders, warehouse lenders, retail lenders, settlement agents, document custodians, title companies, investors, insurers, and country recorders. MERS claims that the consumer benefit as well, though this has been in question until recently.

Ironically, a recent situation has arisen surrounding MERS that may actually benefit many consumers in the end. They are embroiled in the middle of a scandal surrounding original titles and signed promissory notes. Part of what they accomplished in their paperless process led to the loss of such critical original signature documents that the majority of states require for enacting mortgage foreclosures. MERS is now right in the middle of a number of legal challenges resulting from the sub prime crisis and going on in most states around the country. Their right to begin the process of foreclosure has been called into account, since they lack these required original signed documents.

This means that their role in the early days of setting up the system that helped with the buying and selling of mortgages may come back to haunt them and the entire mortgage industry as a whole in the end. Should judges rule these legal suits in favor of the homeowners who took out the mortgages, then it is widely believed that the losses that the banking industry in America suffers from will be so great that they will require substantial amounts of re-capitalization.

Mortgage

Mortgages are loans made on commercial or residential properties. They commonly use the house or the property itself as collateral. These mortgages are paid off in monthly installments over the course of a pre determined amount of time. Mortgages commonly come in fifteen, twenty, and thirty year periods, though both longer ones and shorter ones are available.

A variety of differing mortgages exist. All of them have their own terms and conditions that translate into advantages and disadvantages. Among the various mortgage types are fixed rate mortgages, adjustable rate mortgages, and balloon payment mortgages.

The most common kinds or mortgages, especially for first time home buyers, prove to be fixed rate mortgages. This is the case because they are both simple to understand and extremely stable. With such a mortgage, the regular monthly payments will be the same during the entire life of the loan. This makes them very predictable and manageable. Fixed rate mortgages have the advantages of protection against inflation, since the interest rate is locked in and can not go up with the floating interest rates. They allow for longer term planning. They come with very low risk, since you are always aware of both the payment and interest rate.

Adjustable rate mortgages, also known as ARM's, have become more popular since they begin with lower, more manageable interest rates that result in a lower initial monthly payment. The downside to them is that the interest rate can and likely will go up and down in the loan's life time. Factors to consider with ARM's are the adjustment periods, the indexes and margins, and the caps ceilings, and floors. The adjustment period is the one in which the interest rate is allowed to reset, commonly starting anywhere from six months to ten years after the mortgage begins.

The interest rates change based on the index and margin. The interest rates are actually based on an index that is published, whether it is the London Interbank Offered Rate, or LIBOR, or the U.S. Constant Maturity Treasury, or CMT. The margin is added to this index to determine the total new interest rate on your mortgage. The amount that these ARM rates are capable of going up or down in a single adjustment period and for the life of the loan is called a cap, a ceiling or a floor.

The third common type of mortgages is balloon reset mortgages. They come with thirty year schedules for repayment, with a caveat. Unless you pay are willing to allow the mortgage to reset to then current interest rates at the end of either a five year or seven year term, then your entire balance will be due at this point. This gives you the benefits of the low monthly payment plan as a person with a thirty year loan would have, yet you will have to be willing to pay off the whole mortgage if you do not take the reset option when the term is up. Because of this, many people refer to this type of a mortgage as a two step mortgage.

Mortgage Backed Obligations (MBO)

Mortgage Backed Obligations are also called mortgage backed securities, or MBS. These are real estate-based financial instruments. They represent an ownership stake in a pool of mortgages. They can also be called a financial security or obligation for which mortgages underlie the instrument.

Such a security offers one of three different means for the investor getting paid. It might be that the loan becomes paid back utilizing principal and interest payments that come in on the pool of mortgages which back the instrument. This would make them pass through securities. A second option is that the security issuer could provide payments to the investing party independently of the incoming cash flow off of the borrowers. This would then be a non-pass through security. The third type of security is sometimes referred to as a modified-pass through security. These securities provide the security owners with a guaranteed interest payment each month. This happens whether or not the underlying incoming principal and interest payments prove to be sufficient to cover them or not.

Pass-through securities are not like non-pass through securities in key ways. The pass through ones do not stay on the issuer of the securities' or originators' balance sheets. Non-pass through securities do stay on the relevant balance sheet. With these non pass through variants, the securities are most frequently bonds. These became mortgage backed bonds. Investors in the non-pass through types often receive extra collateral as a letter of credit, guarantees, or more equity capital. This type of credit enhancement is delivered by the insurer of the mortgage backed obligation. The holder of the MBO will be able to count on the security which underlies the instruments in the event that the repayments the pools of mortgages make are not enough to cover the payments (or fail altogether) for the bond holder investors.

These offerings of Mortgage Backed Obligations, Mortgage Backed Bonds, or Mortgage Backed Securities are all ultimately backed up by mortgage pools. Analysts and investors usually call these securitized mortgage offerings. When such types of investments are instead backed up by different kinds of assets and collateral then they have another name. An example of this is the Asset Backed Securities or Asset Backed Bonds.

They are backed up with such collateral as car loans, credit card receivables, or even mobile home loans. Sometimes they are referred to as Asset Backed Commercial Paper when the loans that underlie them are short term loan pools.

With these Mortgage Backed Obligations, they are often grouped together by both risk level and maturity dates. Issuers, investors, and analysts refer to this grouping as tranches, which are the risk profile-organized groups of mortgages. These complicated financial instrument tranches come with various interest rates, mortgage principle balances, dates of maturity, and possibilities of defaulting on their repayments. They are also highly sensitive to any changes in the market interest rates. Other economic scenarios can dramatically impact them as well. This is particularly true of refinance rates, rates of foreclosure, and the home selling rates.

It helps to look at a real world example to understand the complexity of Mortgage Backed Obligations and Collateralized Mortgage Obligations like these. If John buys an MBO or CMO that is comprised of literally thousands of different mortgages, then he has real potential for profit. This comes down to whether or not the various mortgage holders pay back their mortgages. If just a couple of the mortgage-paying homeowners do not pay their mortgages while the rest cover their payments as expected, then John will recover not only his principal but also interest. On the other hand, if hundreds or even thousands of mortgage holders default on their payments and then fall into foreclosure, the MBO will sustain heavy losses and will be unable to pay out the promised returns of interest and even the original principal to John.

Mortgage Backed Securities (MBS)

Mortgage backed securities turn out to be a special kind of asset which have underlying collections of mortgages or individual mortgages that back them. To be qualified as an MBS, the security also has to be qualified as rated in one of two top tier ratings. Credit ratings agencies determine these ratings levels.

These securities generally pay out set payments from time to time which are much like coupon payments. Another requirement of MBS is that the mortgages underlying them have to come from an authorized and regulated bank or financial institution.

Sometimes mortgage backed securities are called by other names. These include mortgage pass through or mortgage related securities. Interested investors buy or sell them via brokers. The investments have fairly steep minimums. These are generally $10,000. There is some variation in minimum amounts depending on which entity issues them.

Issuers are either a GSE Government Sponsored Enterprise, an agency company of the federal government, or an independent financial company. Some people believe that government sponsored enterprise MBS come with less risk. The truth is that default and credit risks are always prevalent. The government has no obligation to bail out the GSEs when they are in danger of default.

Investors who put their money into these mortgage backed securities lend their money to a business or home buyer. Using an MBS, regional banks which are smaller may confidently lend money to their clients without being concerned whether the customers can cover the loan itself. Thanks to the mortgage backed securities, banks are only serving as middlemen between investment markets and actual home buyers.

These MBS securities are a way for shareholders to obtain principal and interest payments out of mortgage pools. The payments themselves can be distinguished as different securities classes. This all depends on how risky the various underlying mortgages are rated within the MBS.

The two most frequent kinds of mortgage backed securities turn out to be collateralized mortgage obligations (CMOs) and pass throughs. Collateralized mortgage obligations are comprised of many different pools of securities. These are referred to as tranches, or pieces. Tranches receive credit ratings. It is these credit ratings which decide what rates the investors will receive. The securities within a senior secured tranche will generally feature lesser interest rates than others which comprise the non secured tranche. This is because there is little actual risk involved with senior secured tranches.

Pass throughs on the other hand are set up like a trust. These trust structures collect and then pass on the mortgage payments to the investors. The maturities with these kinds of pass throughs commonly are 30, 15, or five years. Both fixed rate mortgages and adjustable rate ones can be pooled together to make a pass through MBS.

The pass throughs average life spans may end up being less than the maturity which they state. This all depends on the amount of principal payments which the underlying mortgage holders in the pool make. If they pay larger payments than required on their monthly mortgages, then these pass through mortgages could mature faster.

Mortgage Broker

A mortgage broker is a firm or sole proprietorship that performs a role as an intermediary between banks and businesses or individuals who are looking for mortgage loans. Even though banks have always vended their own mortgage products, mortgage brokers have gradually taken a larger and larger share of the loan originating market as they seek out direct lenders and banks that have the specific products that a customer wants or needs.

Nowadays, sixty-eight percent of all loans begin with mortgage brokers in the United States, making them by far and away the biggest vendors of mortgage products for banks and lenders. The remaining thirty-two percent of loans come from banks own direct marketing efforts and retail branch efforts. Mortgage broker fees are separate from the bank mortgage fees. They are based on the loans' amounts themselves and range from commonly one to three percent of the total loan amount.

Mortgage brokers are mostly regulated in order to make sure that they comply with finance laws and banking rules in the consumer's jurisdiction. This level of regulation does vary per state. Forty-nine of the fifty states have their own laws or boards that regulate mortgage lending within their state's borders. The industry is similarly governed by ten different federal laws that are applied by five federal agencies for enforcement.

Banks find mortgage brokers to be an ideal means of bringing in borrowers who will qualify for a loan. In this way, a mortgage broker acts as a screening agent for a bank. Banks are furthermore able to shift forward a portion of the fraud and foreclosure risks to the loan originators using their contractual legal arrangements with them. In the originating of a loan, a mortgage broker will do the footwork of collecting and processing all of the necessary paper work associated with real estate mortgages.

Mortgage brokers should not be confused with loan officers of a bank. Mortgage brokers are typically state registered and also licensed in order to work as a mortgage broker. This makes them liable personally for any fraud that they commit during the entire life span of the loans in question. Being a mortgage broker comes with professional, legal, and ethical responsibilities that include proper disclosure of mortgage terms to consumers.

Mortgage brokers come with all kinds of experience, as do loan officers, who are employees of banks. While loan officers commonly close more loans than mortgage brokers actually do because of their extensive network of referrals within the bank for which they work, the majority of mortgage brokers make more money than loan officers make. Mortgage brokers generate the lion's share of all loan originations within the country as well.

Mortgage brokers are all represented by the NAMB, which is the acronym for their group the National Association of Mortgage Brokers. The NAMB's mission is to represent the industry of mortgage brokers throughout the U.S. It also offers education, resources to members, and a certification program as well.

Mortgage Costs

Mortgage costs are fees that real estate transactions incur when it is time for them to close. The point for closing comes as the seller transfers the title to the property over to the buyer. Mortgage costs can be absorbed by the seller or the buyer. A number of different expenses go into these overall costs.

The amount for mortgage costs ranges dramatically based on the property the individuals are buying and where they live. They cover many different expenses. There are fees for such things as credit reports, attorney costs, and appraisals. A survey fee pays for the expense of confirming where the property lines are. Pest inspection fees pay to check for termites and other home damaging insects.

Credit report fees pay for running the borrower's credit. Inspections may be requested by the lender or the buyer, and there is a fee for these. With the loan origination fee, lenders receive their compensation for handling all of the loan paperwork on behalf of the borrower. They receive a separate amount called an underwriting fee when they evaluate the application for the mortgage loan.

Other mortgage costs have to do with discounts, titles, and escrows. Discount points turn out to be optional fees that borrowers pay to receive a more favorable interest rate on the loan. A title search fee pays to have a background check performed on the title to ensure that there are no problems like tax liens or unpaid mortgages attached to the property.

Lenders also insist on title insurance. This insurance protects them against a title that turns out not to be clear. The recording fee goes to the county or city to compensate them for adding the update to the land records. There could also be an escrow deposit. This provides for several months of the private mortgage insurance and property tax costs.

Even though mortgage costs vary wildly from one region to another, it is still possible to estimate how high they will be. Home buyers can anticipate commonly paying somewhere between two percent and five percent of the final price of the house in closing fees. This means that if a house costs

$200,000, the mortgage costs could run from $4,000 to $10,000.

The law requires that lenders provide home buyers with a Loan Estimate that covers the amount that these fees will approximately be. They must do this in three days or less of accepting the loan application. These are estimates that will change on a number of the fees.

Three business days or more before the closing occurs, the lender will provide borrowers with a Closing Disclosure statement. This covers the actual closing fees. It is a good idea to hold this up to the original Loan Estimate to contrast the expenses. The lender should explain every item on the fees, why they are important, and why they differed from the original estimate.

In many cases, a significant number of these costs can be negotiated. Some of them can even be removed as unnecessary. This includes fees such as courier, mailing, and administrative costs that the lender is attempting to collect. Borrowers always have the option of walking away from this particular loan if the fees seem high and unreasonable. Other lenders will be agreeable to provide competitive loans with more reasonable fees.

There are also no closing cost mortgages. In these, borrowers are able to sidestep the fees upfront when they close on the loan. Lenders still make money by exacting a higher interest rate or by rolling the costs into the whole mortgage. This last method causes borrowers to pay interest for the mortgage costs as well. Sellers can occasionally be persuaded to absorb the fees at closing.

Mortgage Insurance

Mortgage Insurance refers to a policy that helps would-be homeowners to buy a house with a smaller amount of down payment than traditional bank mortgages require upfront. It is these large typically 20 percent down payments that keep many people from the American dream of home ownership. Such insurance is also known by its popular acronym MI.

Thanks to private mortgage insurance, individuals are able to buy a house and put down a smaller amount than 20 percent. Most lenders and investors alike will insist on such mortgage insurance on any down payment that amounts to under 20 percent. Such MI gives lenders the peace of mind and financial backing that if a loan falls into foreclosure, they will receive financial compensation. This kind of guarantee helps many (if not most) lenders to work with less than the standard 20 percent down payment in home loan scenarios.

The real world application of such MI happens like this. A home buyer wants to purchase a $200,000 house. He is only able to put down 10 percent, amounting to $20,000, for his down payment. The lender will then get the privately issued mortgage insurance on the remaining $180,000 which is the mortgage amount. This will reduce the lender's total exposure from $180,000 down to $150,000. This is because the MI will cover the top 25 percent to 30 percent of the mortgage amount. In this example, the MI has protected 25 percent, or $30,000 beyond the $20,000 down payment, from any end-losses the lender would take in the event of foreclosure on the house. Meanwhile the monthly premiums will become a part of the monthly mortgage payment amount, added on to the monthly amount due for the mortgage repayment.

There can be no doubt of the clear advantages this offers lenders. Yet home buyers also gain from MI in several important ways. The first of these is that they are able to purchase a house far sooner than they would be able to otherwise if they had to save an entire 20 percent standard down payment up themselves. It also boosts their ultimate buying power since they are no longer required to put down a full 20 percent. It is partially refundable according to a pro-rated schedule of premiums when it is cancelled through selling the house before the mortgage has been paid off.

PMI helps to secure quicker approvals for home buyers. Finally, home buyers gain greater cash flow alternatives and flexibility on money that they do not have to put down at closing and tie up with the purchase of the house.

Most MI policies are allowed by the lender to be cancelled out after the loan balance declines to less than 75 percent to 80 percent of the total value of the house. The associated premiums also can be paid according to flexible means with many policies. Some will allow buyers to pay for part or even the entire premium in an initial lump sum during closing so that the monthly premiums will be lower. In either case, the policy can be cancelled when it is no longer needed or the buyer sells the house and pays off the mortgage in the process.

Some lenders will offer to pay the MI premium on the behalf of the home buyer. This is rarely done for free however. The tradeoff to the home buyer is that the lender will boost either the interest rate throughout the life of the mortgage loan or the fees they assess at closing time. This is why it is so critical to understand what the costs are when a lender offers to cover the premium on private mortgage insurance.

Mortgage Modification Package

Mortgage Modification Package refers to an agreement that reduces the homeowners' mortgage payments and possibly overall mortgage debt when they are suffering from significant financial struggles. The idea is to help the borrowers become capable of making their loan payments. This way they can keep their home and not forfeit it in costly foreclosure proceedings.

This does not mean that it is easy to get approved on a Mortgage Modification Package. The mortgage company ultimately will determine if they will allow for such a modification. These changes to the mortgage agreements really are to the advantage of the lender and are often in their best interest. Through helping borrowers to make their payments in a timely fashion, the financial institutions get to keep performing loans and sidestep the tremendous costs, time, and hassle of foreclosing on the property.

The name Mortgage Modification Package describes precisely what occurs in these arrangements. Current mortgage terms become modified so that the interest rate, payments, and overall final balance of the loan are manageable for the borrowers' in question. Amounts which are past due can be paid down either utilizing installments or otherwise can be deferred to the end point of the mortgage. The repayment timeframe of the loan can be extended as well. This lowers the principle payments which are due each month. There are cases where the financial institution will even consent to writing down the remaining loan principle to a manageable amount the borrower can truly afford.

Sometimes these modifications will be temporary. This is often the case where interest rates alone are lowered. They may provide a several year break in the rate that will finally rise back to its original amount. Other times, the lender will permit the borrowers additional time to catch up the late payments without incurring additional fines and fees.

In other scenarios, these modifications can be permanent. This is more common when the financial institutions opt to push out the loan repayment schedule or agree to write down some of the principle which borrowers owe on the mortgage. Without a doubt, such permanent changes to a mortgage are not as easy to receive as are the more temporary in nature ones.

It is not necessarily the financial institution which issued the mortgage loan in the first place which has to approve such a Mortgage Modification Package. Rather the loan servicer is the entity responsible for changing the terms of the loan. This is often another company from the one which extended the mortgage loan upfront.

Loan modifications should never be confused with refinancing, even though they have some similar end results. Both routes will make the payments more affordable in most cases. Yet in order to successfully achieve refinancing, the borrowers will require solid credit and dependable finances. In fact the majority of applicants for loan modifications do not enjoy these significant advantages.

Refinancing is instead actually closing out the existing loan and re-making a new mortgage with which to replace it. The new terms will be more beneficial. Even as borrowers had to qualify for the first mortgage, they must re-qualify for the new one. For some borrowers who are late on or are missing payments altogether (because finances are no longer sufficient to cover the obligations of the mortgage), this will practically rule out qualifying for a traditional refinancing offer.

Mortgage Modification Packages alternatively were purposefully established for those individuals who find themselves in financial straights. They will change the existing mortgage terms in order to help the borrower catch up on late payments and possibly to help make the mortgage terms overall more manageable. This arrangement can be either permanent or temporary.

Mortgage Servicing

Mortgage servicing refers to the organization that handles the administration of a given mortgage loan. When many individuals obtain a mortgage, they mistakenly believe that their lender is going to keep and service this loan until they repay it in full or alternatively sell the house. This is not true much of the time, if not most of the time. In the competitive mortgage market of today, the loans a bank makes and its rights to service them it will commonly sell or buy. This simply means that in many instances, individuals send their payments in to a different company than the one which actually holds their loan.

It is useful to understand the definition of a mortgage servicer. These entities carry the responsibility of managing the daily needs for a given account on a mortgage loan. This includes a number of different services which they perform for the loan. The mortgage servicing model includes receiving and applying the every-month loan installment payments. Servicers also manage the escrow account for any mortgage that possesses one. It is this servicer who homeowners will call or email if they have questions regarding the mortgage itself or any particulars of the loan account.

This administration involved in mortgage servicing revolves around administering the loan from the time the loan proceeds are paid out all the way through the repayment of the loan in full. Besides the obvious tasks that a servicer will perform on a mortgage account, there are several other critically important ones. The servicer must collect and make payments on both insurance and taxes for the borrower. They have to deliver the received funds to the holder of the mortgage. Finally, they have the unpleasant but necessary task of dealing with any delinquencies on the mortgage accounts.

The mortgage servicers receive their compensation for these services in a particular way. They get to keep a fairly small percentage of every loan installment payment. This is called the servicing strip or servicing fee. It typically amounts to between .25% and .5% of the amount of the periodic interest payment.

Looking at an example of how this compensation works out in practice is helpful. When a remaining balance on a given mortgage proves to be $200,000 and there is a servicing fee amounting to .50%, the mortgage servicer will keep .005 divided by 12 months times $200,000 to arrive at a servicing amount of $80. They will retain this $80 from the coming periodic payment and then turn in the rest of the payment amount to the holder of the mortgage.

These mortgage servicing rights can be bought and sold on the secondary market. This happens in a similar fashion to the MBS mortgage backed securities trading. In fact, the mortgage loan servicing value works out to be much like the MBS IO strips value. This is referred to as MSR Mortgage Servicing Rights. Such servicing rights are actually contracted. They provide the rights to service the original mortgage. The initial lender will often sell these off to another firm that specializes in servicing mortgages. The contract will then specify what percentage amount the servicer will keep from each payment.

Though it is hard to believe, the United States national banking laws permit these lending institutions to sell their mortgages and/or servicing rights to any other institution they wish without having to first obtain the consent of the borrower or even to alert them of the change. This is because the interest rate, payment amount, kind of loan, and other terms will stay the same regardless of who services the mortgage. The only difference is that the company and address where the borrower sends the payments will be different.

Lenders might choose to sell these mortgage servicing rights in order to make available additional funds to more borrowers who wish to obtain mortgages. This is necessary as the majority of loans on homes take from 15 to 30 years (or even longer) to repay. Banks would requires billions of dollars in funds to loan out in order to meet the mortgage market demand if they had to keep all of their loans on the books ad infinitum. By selling the loans and/or servicing rights, they are able to help more individuals into homes.

Net Present Value (NPV)

Net Present Value refers to a principal profitability measure that companies utilize in their corporate budget planning process. It helps them to analyze the possible ROI return on investment for a particular proposed or working project. Thanks to the involvement of time value and its depreciating effect on dollars, the NPV is forced to consider a discount rate and its compounding effect throughout the term of the entire project.

The actual Net Present Value in an investment or business project considers the point where revenue (or cash inflow) is equal to or greater than the total investment capital that funds the project or asset in the first place. This is particularly useful for businesses when they are comparing and contrasting a number of different projects or potential projects. It allows them to draw a valuable comparison of their comparative profitability levels to make sure that they only spend their limited resources, time, and management skills on the most valuable ventures. The higher the NPV proves to be, the more profitable it is as an investment, property, or project in the end.

Another way of thinking about the Net Present Value is as a measurement of how well an investment is meeting a targeted yield considering the upfront investment that the firm made. Using this NPV, companies can also determine precisely what adjustment they need in the initial investment in order to reach the hoped for yield. This assumes that all else remains constant.

Net Present Value can also be utilized to effectively visualize and quantify investments in real estate and other asset purchases in a simple formulaic expression. This is that the NPV is equal to the Current value minus the cost. In this iteration of the NPV, the current value of all anticipated future cash flow is discounted to today utilizing the relevant discount rate minus the cost of acquiring said cash flow. This makes NPV essentially the value of the project less the cost. When analysts or corporate accountants examine the NPV in this light, it becomes easy to understand how the value explains if the item being purchased (or project being funded) is more or less valuable than the cost of it in the first place.

Only three total categories of NPV ultimate values are possible for any property purchase or project funding. NPV could be a positive Net Present Value. This means that the buyers will pay less than the true value of the asset. The NPV might also be a Zero NPV. This simply means that the buyer or project funder is paying precisely the value of the asset or project worth. With a negative NPV in the final categorization, the buyer will be paying too much for the asset technically. This will be more than the asset is actually worth. There are cases where companies or buyers might be willing to pursue a project or acquire an asset with a negative NPV when other factors come into play.

For example, they might be interested in purchasing a property for a new corporate headquarters whose NPV is negative. The reasoning behind such a decision could be the unquantifiable and intangible value of the location of the property either for visibility purposes or because it is next to the present company headquarter premises.

It is always helpful to look at a concrete example to de-mystify difficult concepts like Net Present Value. Consider a corporation that wishes to fully analyze the anticipated profits in a project. This given project might need an upfront $10,000 investment to get it off the ground. In three years time, the project is forecast to create revenues amounting to $2,000, $8,000, and $12,000. This means that the project is expected to provide $22,000 on the initial $10,000 outlay.

It would appear that the return will amount to 120 percent for a gain greater than the initial investment. There is a reason why this is not the case though. The discount rate for the time value of money has to be factored in, and this means a percentage of several points per year at least. The figure of 4.5 percent is often utilized on a three year project like this. This takes into consideration the fact that dollars earned three years from now will not be so valuable as today's earned dollars. This is why the corporate accountants will use business calculators in order to plug in the discount time value rates to figure the true NPV. Discounting by the 4.5 percent means that the project actually will return somewhere near $21,000 in terms of today's dollar value.

Origination Fees

Origination fees are also known as activation fees. These are the costs pertaining to setting up an account with a mortgage broker, bank, or other firm that will go through the tasks of collecting and processing all documents and requirements for getting a loan, in particular a mortgage on a house.

These origination fees are generally amounts that are pre determined for any new account. Origination fees can range from half a percentage point to two percentage points of the entire loan total. This variance has to do with where the loans come from, off of either the prime or the subprime loan market. On a subprime mortgage for $200,000, the origination fee would likely amount to two percent, equaling four thousand dollars in this particular case.

The average origination fee comes in at approximately one percent of the total mortgage loan dollar amount. This fee goes to the firm that originates and processes your loan. It defrays their expenses that arise from developing, putting together, and finally closing on your mortgage.

The rise of the Internet has allowed for an alternative compensation scheme for companies that put together and originate mortgages. While the vast majority of mortgage brokers and banks still charge these loan origination fees, there are some Internet based brokers who use a different model. These entities do no charge origination fees at all; instead they pass the savings directly on to you the customer. The way that they get paid is by selling your loan to an investor once it is closed. The investor pays them a premium for the packaged loan, which covers the origination fees, and the online mortgage broker is compensated for his or her work and time.

The origination fees can be deducted from taxes. The year that the transaction closed and the origination fees were charged, they can be used to reduce actual income on income tax forms. The Internal Revenue Service permits this reduction to income no matter who pays the origination fees, meaning that a person who employs a broker that does not charge them origination fees will still be able to deduct the fees that the investors who later buy the loan are subsequently paying to the mortgage broker.

This means that if you take out a $200,000 mortgage, then you are able to deduct the $2,000 in loan origination fees, even if you did not have to pay them, but an investor in the loan did instead.

Origination fees are listed on the HUD-1 Settlement form. They are tallied beneath the sub-heading of lender charges. Discount points that are used to bring down interest rates either permanently or temporarily are also listed on this form under the category.

Owner Financing

Owner Financing refers to the seller carrying all or part of the house sale purchase price. The exception is the amount which the buyer offers by way of down payment. The seller provides the actual financing in this type of a home sale transaction. It is not important if the property already carried a loan when the transaction occurred.

There is always the possibility that the existing lender might find out about the sale and accelerate the loan on the sale utilizing an existing alienation clause contained in the original mortgage contract. Rather than the buyer going to a bank for the purchase price money, the buyer provides their financing instrument to the selling party as proof of the loan. They then make their payments directly to the home seller.

If the property turns out to be unencumbered by an existing loan, then the seller possesses a free and clear title that does not have any current loans. This would permit the seller to freely consent to carrying the entire financing directly with the buyer in this case. In such a scenario, the seller and buyer negotiate and directly settle on an interest rate, term of the loan, and monthly payment amount. The buyer will then pay the seller for the equity in the form of installment payments each month.

Next the security instrument will be recorded within the appropriate public records. This safeguards the interests of the two parties in the transaction. There are states and state regulations which outlaw balloon payment arrangements. It is also important to keep in mind that there are similarly federal government legislations that may govern types of owner-provided financing. This is why it is advisable to seek out legal counsel in order to properly follow the letter of the law in such a transaction and owner arranged financing.

Such purchase types of transactions are freely negotiable. Buyers and seller have the right to come up with their own mutually agreed on methods of financing, assuming that usury laws are not violated nor any other kinds of state- or federal-applicable regulations. The truth is that there is no set amount of down payment mandated in such a private party arrangement. The majority of sellers will want to obtain at least a significant down payment in order to protect their equity in the property though. These might range from next to nothing to as high as even over 30 percent of the total sale price. This safeguards their equity as the buyer is far less likely to walk away from a property into which they have poured even tens of thousands of dollars of their own hard-earned money.

There are a number of variations on the idea of Owner Financing. Promissory Notes allow for the seller to continue carrying their mortgage for the remainder of the loan term on the mortgage. This could be for the whole balance minus the down payment. Such a financing arrangement is known as an all-inclusive mortgage or alternatively as an AITD all-inclusive trust deed.

Land contracts happen when the buyer obtains equitable title but not legal title to the property in question. The buyer still gives payments to the seller for a preset amount of time. Once the last payment is made or a refinance is secured, the buyer receives the actual deed.

Lease Purchase Agreements are another type of Owner Financing. When a seller engages in a sale using a lease purchase agreement this signifies that the seller is providing the buyer with an equitable title and leasing out the property to the purchaser. Once the lease purchase agreement has been completely fulfilled, the buyer gets the title as well as a loan with which to pay the seller. The buyer would obtain credit for part or all of the rental payments which they made toward the contracted purchase price.

Passive Income

Passive income refers to money that, once it is arranged and established, does not require additional work from the person getting it. A variety of different types of passive income exist. Among them are movie, music, book, screenplay, television, and patent royalties. Other samples of passive income include click through income, rental income, and revenue from online advertising.

Activities that lead to passive income have something in common. They usually need a great amount of money, time, or both invested in them upfront to get them started. There are financial means to establishing passive income as well. You could purchase a rental property or choose to invest in a partnership or other form of company where you are a silent partner. The income that you derive from these investment activities is deemed to be passive.

Various other kinds of passive income do not need a great deal of financial investment made in them, but instead require great amounts of effort, time, and even creativity to achieve. More than a year can be required to either build up a popular website that can contribute passive income from advertising or to write a great novel. Making money from such passive income that is actually profit may take longer.

Books are a good example of how long it can take to actually make money from passive income. Publishers generally get to recover all of their printing and promoting costs, as well as any advance monies given to authors, before royalties are created and paid. Books that sell poorly could turn out to pay the author little to nothing.

Websites have a different set of challenges for their creators. There has to be more than simply good content to make money from them. They must similarly rank high in the search engine results for the necessary amount of visitors to find and go to the website. Unless a great number of visitor hits are recorded on a website, the passive income that is generated will be negligible or even none.

People are willing to put in such a huge amount of time with little assurance of results because they know that the passive income generating activity will create money for them around the clock for years to come, if it is successful. This means that passive income money is constantly being made, even when the person is asleep or on vacation. If you are able to get one passive income project up and running well, then you can attempt others. This way, you might hope to develop a few different income streams that result in a significant annual revenue which can even support you.

Many investors believe that passive income is the most superior kind that you can achieve. This is why rental properties can be so popular. Even though they can require a significant amount of maintenance work and tenant management, they can provide substantial income once several such properties are owned and made profitable.

Personal Assets

Personal assets are items of value that belong to an individual. There are many examples of such tangible personal assets. Among these are houses, real estate, cars, and jewelry. Personal assets can also be any other thing with cash value.

When individuals go to a bank or other institution to apply for loans, such personal assets and their values are often considered. These assets are also the bedrock of the formula for net worth for consumers. The value of people's personal assets can be higher than they expect and surprise them as so many different items can be included under this label.

There are many personal assets that are material and easy to measure. These include such financial assets as savings accounts, checking accounts, and retirement accounts. Assets that have a value that can not be easily accessed are also included in the personal assets category. This includes life insurance policies and annuities that have cash values. Other items of value which would be included in a list of personal assets cover such items as antiques, art collections, electronics, personally owned businesses, and other valuable items.

Personal assets can do more than simply help people get loans and count towards net worth. They are also sometimes able to create income for their owners. Bank accounts and savings accounts accrue interest. Holders of real estate are able to lease or rent it out. This brings in rent or lease fees. Individuals who have personal assets should educate themselves in the best practices for managing them so that they are able to increase their total wealth by generating the highest income possible from them.

It is important to keep a careful track of rent or other income obtained from personal assets as the money will be taxable. Income that is not properly reported to the government on the correct tax forms can incur penalties from the Internal Revenue Service.

It is also important to know the value of an individual's personal assets. There are two different methods of learning this. In the first method, individuals examine the item's market value. This is the value for which the asset would sell if a person were to put it straight on the market. Another way to determine the value of these assets is to have a personal asset appraised.

Appraised values can be substantially greater than market values. This is because an appraisal value relies on the possible future price of the item in question. This difference matter significantly, particularly when having an item insured. Individuals generally have to obtain appraised value insurance coverage. This means that they will likely have to pay for a greater amount of insurance.

When properly managed, personal assets can greatly contribute to an individual's personal financial situation. It is also true that these assets can prove to be a liability if they are not well taken care of or managed. Part of managing assets well involves asset allocation.

Financial experts warn against placing all or the majority of personal assets into a single asset type or location. This type of practice causes people to take on additional risk than is prudent. Instead, it is better to spread around an individual's wealth into a variety of different assets so that if one suffers or decreases in value, some of the other assets may offset this by outperforming or increasing in value.

Taking care of personal assets is also an important part of maintaining their value. Individuals can break expensive electronics if they are not careful. Not engaging in proper maintenance for works of art can also lead to their value declining over time.

Portfolio

In the world of business and finance, a portfolio stands for an investment collection that a person or institution holds. People and other entities put together portfolios in order to diversify their holdings to reduce risk to a manageable level. A number of different kinds of risk are mitigated through the acquisition of a few varying types of assets. A portfolio's assets might be comprised of stocks, options, bonds, bank accounts, gold certificates, warrants, futures contracts, real estate, facilities of production, and other assets that tend to hold their value.

Investment portfolios may be constructed in various ways. Financial entities will commonly do their own careful analysis of investments in putting together a portfolio. Individuals might work with the either financial firms or financial advisors that manage portfolios. Alternatively, they could put together a self directed portfolio through working with a self directed online broker such as TD Ameritrade, eTrade, or Scott Trade.

A whole field of portfolio management has arisen to help with the allocation of investment money. This management pertains to determining the types of assets that are appropriate for an individual's risk tolerance and ultimate goals. Choosing the instruments that will comprise a portfolio has much to do with knowing the kinds of instruments to buy and sell, how many of each to obtain, and the time that is most appropriate to purchase or sell them.

Such decisions are rooted in a measurement for the investments' performance. This usually pertains to risk versus return on investments and anticipated returns of the entire portfolio. With portfolio returns, various types of assets are understood to commonly return amounts of differing ranges. Portfolio management has to factor in an individual investor's own precise situation and desired results as well. There are investors who are more fearful of risk than are other investors. These kinds of investors are termed risk averse. Risk averse portfolios are significantly different in their composition than are typical portfolios.

Mutual funds have evolved the act of portfolio management almost to a science. Their fund managers came up with techniques that allow them to prioritize and ideally set their portfolio holdings. This fund management reduces risk and increases returns to maximum levels. Strategies that these managers have created for running portfolios include designing equally weighted portfolios, price weighted portfolios, capitalization weighted portfolios, and optimal portfolios in which the risk adjusted return proves to be the highest possible.

Well diversified portfolios will contain many different asset classes. These will include far more than just stocks, bonds, and mutual funds. They will feature international stocks and bonds to provide diversification away from the U.S. dollar, as well as foreign currencies and hard asset commodities such as real estate investments, and gold and silver holdings.

Portfolio Income

Portfolio income proves to be money that is actually brought in from a group of investments. The portfolio commonly includes all of the various types of investments that an investor owns. These include bonds, stocks, mutual funds, and certificates of deposit. These various financial instruments earn a variety of different types of passive income, such as dividends, interest income, and capital gain distributions. Such portfolio income returns are generated by the holdings of the various investment products in the portfolio.

Portfolio income varies with the types of investments that an investor picks. You as an investor will commonly look at two different factors when assembling a portfolio for portfolio income. These turn out to be the money that the investment itself will produce, which is also known as an investment's return, and the investment's risk level that it contains.

As an example, stocks are frequently deemed to be investments with considerable risk, yet the other side of the risk return equation is that they provide income from a company's dividends, or distribution earnings returned to the shareholders, as well as an increase in the stock price as the stock value gains with time. Certificates of deposit and bonds create interest income that is paid out on the investment that you hold. Still different kinds of investments produce other types of income, although this depends on the characteristics of the investment in question.

To maximize the portfolio income while reducing the amount of risk involved, individuals commonly choose to invest in numerous different kinds of investments. This is known as diversifying your portfolio and portfolio income. This way, you can combine both safer investments that provide lower real returns with riskier investments that offer greater investment returns. Your total collection of investments is the portfolio that makes your portfolio income for you.

This portfolio income is also classified as passive income, or income that does not require you to perform any work in order to make the money. The upfront investment actually creates the income without you having to be actively involved in the money making process. This stands in contrast to incomes that are earned through active involvement, or active income that you must expend both energy and time to create.

The ultimate goal for you with your portfolio income will probably be to build up enough of it that you are capable of living off of only the income that the portfolio generates. Once this point is reached, you would be able to not receive a payroll check any longer. Instead, you would support yourself in retirement from the dividends, interest, and capital gains created by the investments in the form of portfolio income. The best and safest way to do this is to only draw on the portfolio income itself, without drawing down the original principal.

By not touching the investment principal, you allow your portfolio and resulting portfolio income to build up over time. If you do not take out the portfolio income, then the total value of the portfolio will grow faster with time, allowing you to compound your investments for retirement. It is critical to have enough money saved for retirement that you do not need to take out this principal to support yourself. Sufficient portfolio income should be generated to cover the monthly retirement expenses. In this way, you will not be reducing your principal and risking the very real danger of your portfolio running out of money while you are still alive to need it.

Prime Rate

The Prime Rate is the most typically utilized shorter term interest rate for the United State banking system. All kinds of lending institutions in the United States employ this U.S. benchmark interest rate as a basis or index rate to price their medium term to short term loans and products. This includes credit unions, thrifts, savings and loans, and commercial banks.

This makes the Prime Rate consistent around the country as banks strive to be competitive and profitable in their lending rates which they provide to both consumers and businesses. A universal rate like this simplifies the task for businesses and consumers as they shop around comparable loan products that competing banks offer. Every state in the country does not maintain its own benchmark rate. This makes a California Prime or New York Prime identical to the U.S. Prime.

Commercial and other banks charge this benchmark rate to their best customers. These are those clients who have the best credit ratings and loan history with the bank. Most of the time banks' best clients are made up of large companies.

The prime interest rate is also known as the prime lending rate. Banks typically base it on the Federal Reserve's federal funds rate. This is actually the rate that banks loan money to each other for overnight purposes. Retail customers also need to be aware of the prime lending rate. It directly impacts the lending rates that they can access for personal and small business loans as well as for home mortgages.

The federal government and Federal Reserve Bank do not set the prime lending rates. The individual banks set it. They then utilize this base rate or reference rate to set the prices for a great number of loans such as credit card loans and small business loans.

The Federal Reserve Board releases a statistics called "Selected Interest Rates." This is their survey of the prime interest rate as the majority of the twenty-five biggest banks set it. It is this publication which reveals the Prime Rate periodically. This is why the Federal Reserve does not directly set this important benchmark rate. The banks more or less base it on the target level of the federal funds rate that the Federal Open Market Committee sets and changes at their monthly meetings.

Different banks adjust their prime lending rate at the same time. The point where they change it is generally when the Federal Open Market Committee adjusts their own important Fed Funds Rate. Many publications refer to this periodically changing reference rate as the Wall Street Prime Rate.

A great number of consumer loans as well as commercial loans and credit card rates find their basis in the prime lending rate. Among these are car loans, home equity loans, personal and home lines of credit, and various kinds of personal loans.

The rates above the prime lending rate that banks charge their less then prime (or subprime) customers depend on the credit worthiness of the borrower in question. The banks attempt to correctly ascertain the risk of default for the borrower. For the best credit customers who have lower chances of defaulting, banks can afford to assess them a lower interest rate than others. Customers with higher chances of defaulting on their loans pay larger interest rates because of the risk associated with their loans not being repaid.

As of June 15, 2016, the Federal Open Market Committee voted to maintain its target fed funds rate in a range of from .25% to .5%. As a result of this, the U.S. prime lending rate stayed at 3.5%. Once per month the Federal Reserve committee meets to determine if they will change the fed funds rate.

Private Equity

Private Equity refers to an investment capital source that comes from those institutional investors and accredited individual investors who boast high net worth. The goals of these investors are to gain a significant equity ownership in corporations. The partners at these firms raise funds and then manage them to gain higher than average returns for their client shareholders. They commonly pursue this goal via an investment time frame of from four to seven years. Private equity is therefore not for those who require that their investment positions be readily liquid.

Such mega funds are often utilized to buy private companies or to privatize publically listed corporations in order to de-list them from the stock market exchanges in a go private arrangement. Each firm sets its own minimum investment threshold for the fund investors. This ranges depending on the needs of the funds being raised. There are many funds with a minimum $250,000 in smallest investment permitted, while still others look for at least millions of dollars per contributing investor.

The private equity industry has a long and storied history of gaining the best possible talent from the corporate world throughout America. This includes top-delivering CEOs and directors even from Fortune 500 firms as well as the best management consulting and top strategy firms. This is why private equity hiring managers often scout out major corporations, law firms, and accounting companies when they go recruiting for new talent. They require legal experience and accounting skills to provide the many support services that such large enterprises require in order to put together major corporate mergers and acquisitions and to properly advise the management companies on the effective management of their newly acquired portfolios holdings.

There are quite high fees involved with such firms. Typically they receive first a management fee and then a performance fee. This generally amounts to annual management fees at around two percent of all assets under management. The performance fees add up to 20 percent of all gross profits when they sell a company. There can be a great deal of variety in the ways that such firms receive their compensation and incentives to outperform.

It is not hard to understand why private equity has been so successful at recruiting and keeping the very best talent based upon the money they have to offer by way of compensation for performance. Consider that these firms which have a billion dollars' assets under management would likely have around only two dozen professional investment personnel. They receive $20 million in annual fees just for the assets under management. Add on to this the 20 percent performance fees based on all gross profits, and it is not hard to understand how they generate additional tens of millions of dollars in performance fees for the company.

Middle market level managers and associates generally expect to earn six-figure salaries and bonuses. The vice presidents pull down half a million dollars easily. Principals rake in a cool over million dollars per year in both realized and unrealized compensation.

Given the incredible rewards at stake, it should not come as any surprise that there are a range of types of private equity firms operating today. Many choose the route of passive investing to be strictly financiers. They depend on their appointed management to increase the size and profitability of the firm in which they invest so that the owners will realize generous, outsized returns. Other kinds of these firms choose to be more active investors. They deliver operational support to the management to ensure that they can build up a stronger and more profitable firm which they can then resell or spin off.

These private equity firms pride themselves on their expansive list of contacts and relationships with corporate boards. They leverage these CFO and CEO relationships to help them grow the company revenue as well as to recognize synergies and operational combination opportunities. One of the kingpins of private equity remains Goldman Sachs, the legendary investment bank. They facilitate the biggest deals and concentrate their time on forging acquisitions and mergers that have billions of dollars in notional values. For other smaller investment banking companies, the majority of deals run in the range of from $50 million to $500 million, while lower middle-market transactions vary from $10 million to $50 million in total.

Private Mortgage Insurance (PMI)

PMI is the acronym for Private Mortgage Insurance, also known sometimes as Lenders Mortgage Insurance. PMI proves to be insurance that is paid to a lending institution that is required much of the time when an individual gets a mortgage loan. Such insurance is used to cover any losses that arise if a person is not capable of paying back their mortgage loan.

Should the lender not be able to recoup all of its costs in foreclosing on and selling the mortgaged property, then PMI insurance covers the remaining losses that exist on the balance sheet of the bank or other lender. The general rates for this Private Mortgage Insurance turn out to be around $55 each month for every $100,000 that is actually financed. On a $250,000 loan, this amounts to $1,875 each year in premiums.

Private Mortgage insurance yearly costs range though. They are usually given out in comparison against the entire loan's value. This depends on a number of factors, such as loan type, loan term, actual coverage amount, amount of home value that the person finances, the premium payment frequency that might be monthly or yearly, and the individual's credit score. While PMI can be paid in advance with closing costs, it can also be worked into the loan payments with single premium PMI.

Private Mortgage Insurance is generally only necessary when the down payment proves to be smaller than twenty percent of either the appraised value of the property or alternatively of the sales price. When then loan to value ratio is greater than eighty percent, you can expect to be required to carry it. As the principal is reduced with monthly payments, or the home value rises through real estate appreciation, or a combination of the two occurs, then this Private Mortgage Insurance might not be required any longer. At this point, the home owner is allowed to discontinue paying for the PMI insurance.

There are some banks and lenders who will insist that PMI be paid for minimally for a pre fixed period of time, such as two to three years. This is regardless of whether the principal value of the property exceeds eighty percent in a shorter amount of time. Banks do not have to permit a person to cancel this insurance legally until the loan has amortized down to a Loan to Value ratio of seventy-eight percent of the original price for which the house is purchased.

A cancellation request must originate from the mortgage servicer. They must send it to the issuing company that made the PMI policy in the first place. Many times, such a mortgage servicer will insist on a current home value appraisal being done in order to ascertain the actual loan to value ratio.

Premiums paid for mortgage insurance were not tax deductible according to the Internal Revenue Service in the past. In 2007 this changed. Now all PMI premiums are considered to be fully reducing of your income for the year in question.

Promissory Note

Promissory notes are negotiable instruments that are called notes payable in accounting circles. In such promissory notes, an issuer writes an unlimited promise that he or she will pay a certain amount of money to the payee. This can be set up either on demand of the payee, or at a pre arranged future point in time. Specific terms are always arranged for the repayment of the debt in the promissory note.

Promissory notes are somewhat like IOU's and yet quite different. Unlike an IOU that only agrees that there is a debt in question, promissory notes are made up of a particular promise to pay the debt. In conversational vernacular, loan contract, loan agreement, or loan are often utilized in place of promissory note, even though such terms do not mean the same things legally. While a promissory note does provide proof of a loan in existence, it is not the loan contract. A loan contract instead has all of the conditions and terms of the particular loan arrangement within it.

Promissory notes contain a variety of term elements in them. Among these are the amount of principal, the rate of interest, the parties involved, the repayment terms, the date, and the date of maturity. From time to time, provisions may be included pertaining to the payee's rights should the issuer default. These rights could include the ability to foreclose on the issuer's assets.

A particular type of promissory note is a Demand Promissory note. This specific kind does not come with an exact date of maturity. Instead, it is due when the lender demands repayment. Generally, in these cases lenders only allow several days advance notice before the payment must be made.

Within the U.S., the Article 3 of the Uniform Commercial Code regulates most promissory notes. These negotiable forms of promissory notes are heavily used along with other documents in mortgages that involve financing purchases of real estate properties. When people make loans in between each other, the making and signing of promissory notes are commonly critical for the purposes of record keeping and paying taxes. Businesses also receive capital via the use of promissory notes that are sometimes referred to as commercial papers. These promissory notes became a finance source for the creditors of the firm receiving money.

Promissory notes have functioned like currency that proved to be privately issued in the past. Because of this, such promissory notes that are bearer negotiable have mostly been made illegal, since they represent an alternative to the officially sanctioned currency. Promissory notes go back to well before the 1500's in Western Europe. Tradition claims that the very first one ever signed existed in Milan in 1325. Reference is made to some being issued between Barcelona and Genoa back in 1384, even though we no longer have the promissory notes themselves. The first one that we still have dates back to 1553 where Ginaldo Giovanni Battista Stroxxi issued one that he created in Medina del Campo, Spain against the city of Besancon.

Short Sale

Short sales are real estate sales where the money received from the sale is not sufficient to cover the balance that is owed on the property loan. This commonly happens as a result of borrowers being unable to keep up with the mortgage payments for their home loan. In this case, the bank or other lending institution will likely determine that it is in their best interest to take a reasonable loss on the sale of the property instead of pressuring the borrower to make the payments that he or she can not afford.

Both parties come together and agree on the short sale process, since it permits them both to stay out of foreclosure. Foreclosure is a negative outcome for the two parties, as it lowers credit scores of borrowers and costs banks in expensive fees. Borrowers must be careful, since a short sale agreement does not always absolve the borrower from having to cover the additional balance left on the loan. This remaining balance is called the deficiency.

The process of a short sale starts with the two parties concurring on a short sale being the best option to resolve a mortgage that the borrower is unable to keep up with as a result of financial or economic difficulties. The home owner actually sells the house in question for an amount that he or she is able to realize, even though it is less than the remaining loan balance. They give the money to the bank or lender. This is really the most economical answer for the problem in this scenario, since short sales are less costly and quicker than foreclosures that damage both lender and borrower.

Banks commonly employ loss mitigation departments. Their job is to contemplate the short sales that are possible or likely. Most of them work with criteria that they have set up in advance. In the difficult days following the financial crisis of 2007-2010, they have become more flexible and willing to entertain offers from borrowers. The banks will usually decide on how much equity is in the house by ascertaining the likely selling price that they will be able to receive either through a Broker Price Opinion, appraisal, or Broker Opinion of Value.

Even when Notice of Defaults have been sent out to borrowers beginning a foreclosure process, many banks will still consent to short sale requests and offers. They have become more understanding and accepting of short sales in the wake of the financial crisis than they ever were before. This means that for the countless borrowers who own houses on which they owe more than they are worth and who can not sell them, there is a better option open to them than foreclosure.

Sub-prime Borrower

A sub-prime borrower is an individual who has credit that is considered to be less than perfect. This is the opposite of a prime borrower. Bankers call prime borrowers those who possess higher and better credit scores, low debt ratios, and significant incomes which are more than enough to cover their monthly bills and expenses.

Sub-prime borrowers often are only able to obtain sub-prime loans. These types of loans received the blame for causing the 2008 mortgage crisis. Despite this fact, the loans continue to exist today. They are an important part of post crisis lending, though so far they have not caused another financial crisis or global meltdown.

Those called sub-prime borrowers have many characteristics in common. These imply that the individuals are more likely to default on their mortgage loans than other individuals. Poor credit is the first element they share. This could be because they did not receive any opportunities to create a sufficient credit history.

It might also be from problems they had with making payments in the past. The dilemma for these borrowers is that they do not have many choices other than sub-prime lenders. This often traps them in a cycle of debt from which is difficult to escape. An under 640 credit score is considered to be sub-prime, though some lenders set the defining limit lower to even 580.

The sub-prime borrowers also have problems with their monthly payments. These payments are so large that they consume a significant part of the monthly income for the borrowers. This is determined in how high the debt to income ratio proves to be. A higher DTI ratio means that the borrowers do not have enough money to cover bills if they suffer a drop in income or have unanticipated expenses arise. Loans can still be approved in some scenarios when the borrowers' present debt load is significant.

The cost for a sub-prime loan is another thing these borrowers share together. These forms of mortgage loans usually cost more since lenders do not want to assume additional risk without higher compensation. Predatory lenders have used this limited ability to receive loan approvals in order to prey on borrowers with no other choices. These higher expenses manifest in a few different ways. It might be junk application and processing fees, greater interest rates, and penalties for early prepayment which prime borrowers seldom pay.

Risk is the dominant theme for sub-prime borrowers, lenders, and loans. Because the loans have a lower chance of being paid back, the lenders exact more in fees and higher rates. These greater costs cause the loans to be riskier for the borrowers as well. Debt is difficult to retire when higher interest rates and costs come with it.

Sub-prime borrowers should try to avoid these expensive and debt trapping loans whenever they can. Staying out of such costly credit is essential for individuals to not drown in debt. This is easier said than done when people are put into the sub-prime category. There are not as many options to comparison shop for the loans. There are also fewer options for alternative kinds of loans to use for the needed financing.

If these borrowers are able to make themselves look less risky to the various lenders, it will improve their chances of escaping from these types of loans. This may mean some credit repair work needs to be done before individuals with credit challenges make applications for loans.

Sub-prime Lender

A sub-prime lender makes loans to customers who fall into the sub-prime borrower category. These products often include loans which are normally considered to be standard. They are structured for and marketed to borrowers who possess inadequate income, lower credit scores, and a higher debt to income ratio. These borrowers can not qualify with lenders regarded as traditional.

Sub-prime lenders are often willing to issue loans to customers with special circumstances. These include those who possess less documentation of income, high LTV loan to value ratios, and sometimes a combination of the two. This type of lending is considered to be aggressive and overly risky for most traditional financial institutions.

Where mortgages are concerned, sub-prime lenders are still providing basically the same product in the form of a 5/1 ARM adjustable rate mortgage or a 30 year fixed rate mortgage. The main difference is that the rate which accompanies such a product will be considerably higher.

There are other types of mortgage loans that some observers include in this category as well. Among these are negative amortization loans, interest only loans, and non fixed interest rate mortgages. A great number of analysts consider FHA loans to be in the subprime category. This is because their highest allowable LTV is 96.5% while they accept a credit score minimum of 500.

Sub-prime lenders will also make loans for other assets and in other categories besides housing and mortgages. In fact they issue them for practically all financing needs. This includes credit cards, car loans, unsecured personal loans, and student loans.

After the financial crisis that started with sub-prime mortgages, the government enacted a number of laws protecting consumers from these predatory types of finance. It has made it more difficult to find sub-prime house loans since then. There are a great many of the original loans from before the crisis still in existence. Besides this, sub-prime lenders have found means of circumventing them and giving approval to loans that fall into this category.

Borrowers can take many actions to avoid being a victim of a sub-prime lender. Managing credit carefully is among the most important. It is free to check all credit reports for accuracy. Borrowers can fix errors. Consumers should also deal with any defaults or missed payments if they can. Rebuilding credit requires some time, but going through the process will help borrowers to be considered more prime to lenders.

There are many newer lenders these days that are considered to be legitimate. Online searches and online lenders have opened a whole new avenue to consumers trying to avoid sub-prime loans. Some of these online lenders appeal to those with poor credit and still provide acceptable rates.

There are also peer to peer lending services. They can be more flexible with borrowers than the traditional credit unions and banks often are. It is always a good idea to research any lenders which consumers consider before providing them with important personal information or paying any fees.

Borrowers who are struggling to avoid these sub-prime lenders can also look into a co-signer on a loan. It can help credit challenged borrowers to receive approval from a lender which is traditional and offers better rates. These co-signers put their own credit at stake and take a big risk in doing so.

Sub-prime Mortgage

A sub-prime mortgage is one where the home loan that the bank or lending institution makes is offered to the category of consumers who are considered to possess the riskiest credit. Sub prime mortgages are actually sold on a different market than are prime mortgage loans. Sub prime mortgage borrowers are determined through a combination of factors, such as the credit rating of the borrower, the documentation offered for the loans, and the borrower's debt to assets ratio. Besides this, sub-prime mortgage are also deemed to be those that do not fulfill the prime mortgages' standards and guide lines offered by Fannie Mae and Freddie Mac, the two biggest issuers of mortgages within the United States.

A universally agreed upon definition for sub-prime mortgages does not exist today. In the U.S., sub-prime mortgages are commonly considered to be those where the associated borrower possesses a FICO credit rating score that is less than 640. This phrase became a part of pop culture in the credit crunch that occurred in 2007.

The original sub-prime mortgage program began in 1993. At this time, some lenders started offering sub-prime mortgages to borrowers classified as high risk, who possessed credit that was less than ideal. Traditional lenders showed wariness towards sub-prime mortgages and borrowers. They tended to shy away from people who had impaired credit histories. Sub-prime mortgage borrowers commonly have information on their credit reports that argue for greater percentages of defaults. These include too much debt, a track record of not paying debts or missing payments, recorded bankruptcies, and low amounts of experience with debt.

Around twenty-five percent of the American population is grouped into this category of sub-prime borrowers who qualify for the category of sub-prime mortgages. Because of this, proponents of sub-prime mortgages argued that they allowed a large number of people to gain access to credit who would not otherwise have experienced the opportunity to purchase and own a home. Borrowers with less than perfect credit who can demonstrate enough income are able to qualify for sub-prime mortgages. This proves to be the case even if their credit scores are lower than 640.

The lenders who participate in sub-prime mortgages take significant risks in so doing. This is because people who have a credit score of less than 620 statistically possess a significantly greater rate of defaulting on their mortgages than do those people with much higher scores over 720. Lenders compensate for the risks associated with offering sub-prime mortgages through several different means. One of these is by charging higher rates of interest. They also collect late fees for any customers who do not keep up with their payments. These greater interest rates and fees help to reward lenders who take the risks of the higher default rates, and who also incur costs for collecting and keeping up with these -mortgage accounts. As an example of their potential danger, sub-prime mortgages proved to be among the main causes of the Financial Crisis of 2007-2010.

Sub-prime Mortgage Crisis

The sub-prime mortgage crisis proves to be a still going financial and real estate crisis. It continues to revolve around the steep decline that you saw in American housing prices, the resulting increase in numbers of mortgage delinquencies and finally foreclosures, and the ultimate fall of securities that are backed up by these sub-prime mortgages.

The problems began with the fact that around eighty percent of all United States mortgages that banks gave out to sub-prime borrowers, or people with less than perfect credit, turned out to be adjustable rate types of mortgages. Housing prices actually reached their highest point in the middle of 2006 and then began sharply falling. This caused refinancing of interest rates on mortgages to be harder to obtain. The double edged sword of adjustable rate mortgages resetting at their higher rates started, causing an enormous number of delinquencies and finally foreclosures in mortgages.

The greater problem came as these mortgages underlay a number of financial securities that many financial firms held in huge numbers. They saw most of their value disappear in the following months. Investors around the world then began to dramatically cut back on the quantities of collateralized debt obligations and other mortgage securities that they bought. Besides the damage that increasing sub-prime mortgage delinquencies and foreclosures created themselves and for the investments based on them, this sub-prime mortgage crisis led to a fall in the ability of the banking system to engage in lending. This caused significantly tighter credit and lower rates of growth throughout the developed world, in particular in Europe and the United States,that are still plaguing the industrial countries.

Ultimately, the sub-prime mortgage crisis arose as a result of easy up front loan terms which banks made to borrowers. Both the borrowers and the banks felt confident that the loans could be easily refinanced into better terms as needed, since housing prices were steadily rising over a long term trend. Financial incentives were provided to sub-prime mortgage originators.

This coupled, with fraud that borrowers and lenders engaged in, significantly boosted the quantities of sub-prime mortgages to customers who should have received standard conforming loans or who should not have received loans at all. When the easy interest rate terms expired, the majority of sub-prime loan holding consumers could not refinance at the better rates in which they had believed. The interest rates reset higher, dramatically increasing the monthly mortgage payments.

Home prices started falling to the point that homes were no longer even worth as much as the original mortgage, meaning that they could not be sold to pay off the mortgage obligation. Instead, the borrowers' best interest lay in going through foreclosure and walking away from the hopelessly underwater homes. This continuous epidemic of foreclosures that began with the sub-prime mortgage crisis is still a major continuous part of the world wide financial and economic crisis. The foreclosures are still taking away wealth from consumers and sapping away at the damaged banks' balance sheets.

Subordinate Financing

Subordinate financing refers to that type of debt finance which ranks behind the primary finance. It is second in importance and position to debt that senior or secured lenders hold. This is important when a default occurs, as it determines who gets repaid first from any bankruptcy proceedings or foreclosure. The term signifies that senior lenders who are secured will be repaid before the debt holders that are subordinate.

Lenders who participate in this subordinate financing take on greater risk than the lenders considered to be senior. This is because they have a lower claim on the business or property assets. Sometimes this type of corporate finance is comprised of both equity and debt financing. A lender would be interested in this because it would offer them potential stock options or warrants that would reward them with extra yield as a means of compensating for the greater risk they take.

Where consumer borrowers and loans are concerned, subordinate financing would be a second mortgage. It takes second priority below the original first mortgage. First mortgages have the property to secure their loan and the debt. While nearly every mortgage is backed by the underlying property, first mortgages receive special seniority ahead of subordinated mortgages. This means the senior mortgage lender is repaid first in a foreclosure. With mortgages, subordinate financing could be a mortgage that is 80/20. In this case, the first mortgage would be 80 percent while the second mortgage that was subordinated represents 20 percent.

This means that only the lenders which are first mortgage holders are likely to get at least a portion of their money back if a borrower defaults in general. Should a borrower only default on the subordinate mortgage, this lender is able to foreclose on the property to regain its principal. Subordinated lenders could work to make their mortgage the senior one and then foreclose. They could do this by buying out their borrower's first mortgage. Afterwards, they could choose to subordinate the original first mortgage so that their once second mortgage became senior in the foreclosure.

Consumers should think carefully before participating in subordinate financing to obtain their houses. There are several disadvantages involved. Home owners will usually have to write two different mortgage payments each month if they do. They will also typically pay a higher interest rate on the second mortgage since these rates are usually greater than the first mortgage rates. There are also often two different loan fees, costs, and even discount points when first and second mortgages are used. Finally, this type of finance will often lead to a greater monthly payment when the two are combined than only one mortgage payment would.

The main reason that a home buyer would be interested in employing subordinated financing to purchase a home is because an 80/20 mortgage would not require them to come up with any down payment. It might also eliminate the need to pay for PMI private mortgage insurance which can be a substantial component of the monthly mortgage payment. This would depend on how the mortgage financing was originally structured.

Consumers will generally require a high credit score of minimally 700 in order to qualify for this subordinated financing. When borrowers have two mortgages, it will likely be impossible to obtain a home equity loan or line of credit at a later time.

Tax Abatement

Tax abatement represents a taxation level reduction. It can be for either individual consumers or companies. There are many examples of this type of tax break. They could be in the form of a rebate, reduction in tax penalties, or an actual tax decrease. Sometimes people or firms pay too many taxes or get a tax bill that is higher than it should be. In this case, they have the right to ask for an abatement from the IRS or state taxing agency.

Among the different types of tax abatement is the property tax kind. Owners of property might feel that their property value is assessed too highly. They would be able to appeal to the area tax assessor to receive a tax abatement. Businesses that are not for profit can obtain them on their property because of their special tax exempt status.

Tax abatement on property is a major savings. Most owners of houses will be required to pay property taxes that are commonly from 1% to 3% of the value of the house every year. This annual expense does not disappear when the mortgage is completely paid. It represents part of the ongoing cost of owning a home.

There are cities that offer special programs of real estate tax abatement. Such a package assists consumers dramatically. It could help them to purchase a nicer house for the same payment. It might also allow them to be able to obtain a mortgage that they might not otherwise. This is the case if the monthly house payment drops to a level they can afford through such abatement. This type of abatement on property can also help to boost the resale value of the house if it is still in effect when the owner sells.

Some cities in the U.S. offer tax abatement's to massively lower or even completely eliminate tax payments on houses for not only years but even decades. The idea behind such a program is to bring in buyers to neighborhoods that are in poor demand. This could be part of the inner city which the city is attempting to revitalize. Cities can offer these abatement's throughout the entire limits. Others provide them for specific areas. Authorities can choose to restrict such programs to middle or low income owners of property as well. A great number of these abatement programs do not carry such an income restriction.

It is possible to purchase properties that are already under abatement. Individuals may also buy properties that are eligible and go through with the necessary improvements. They then apply for this program. It is far easier to buy a property with an abatement than to go through the hassle of bureaucracy and construction.

For abatement's on improvements to a property, there are special rules. The improvement, rehabilitation, or construction property taxes can be reduced or eliminated. This does not mean that the entire property tax is gone. The pre-improved value of the property will still have taxes owed for it in this particular case.

It is often necessary for a house to be occupied by the owner for the abatement to continue. Renting the house out would cause the special status to disappear. When an owner sells a home to another owner who will occupy it, the property tax abatement will stay with the house. Abatement periods never restart just because the property transfers ownership. If a 10 year program eliminates or reduces the taxes on a home and the seller has enjoyed seven of these years, then the new owner will have the three years left of the status.

Title Deed

Title deeds are a form of legal documents. They are utilized to demonstrate that a person owns a certain property. Title deeds are used most often to provide proof of home or vehicle ownership. Title deeds might also be given out on other kinds of property. Title deeds give owners privileges and legal rights. To transfer a property's ownership to another individual, a title deed is required.

Title deeds generally come with detailed descriptions of the property to which they are attached. They are made specific enough so that they can not be mixed up with other properties. They also include the individual's name who owns the piece of property. More than one person can be named as an owner on a title deed. Proof that the title deed is recorded with the appropriate office is provided by the presence of an official seal. Title deeds are commonly signed by the property owner and a person who witnesses the signature, such as a clerk or area government official.

Having a title deed does not mean that a person keeps the car in his or her possession. You can loan a car to a relative to use, even though they are not on the title. If you purchase a car using a loan, then the bank will have the title for its security, even though you would keep the car. You might purchase a house and rent it to a tenant. Although the tenant would not have the title deed, he or she would still possess and occupy the house. The title deed is useful for forcefully retaking possession in any of these scenarios.

When you sell a property, the old title deed is invalidated and a new one is given out that has the new owner's name on it. You might also add another person to a title deed by working with a title company for a property, or the Department of Motor Vehicles for vehicle titles. You have to fill in a request in writing before you receive a new title deed with the other names added to it. Once a person's name has been added to a title deed, they legally control the property along with the original title deed owner.

Title deeds have to be kept safe. As official legal documents, they are not easy to replace when stolen or lost. It is a smart idea to keep title deed copies separate from the original to have proof of ownership while an official replacement title deed is being issued. Physical possession of title deeds allows a person to start a transfer of ownership, so they must be kept where they will not be stolen and then subsequently utilized to transfer your property to another individual.

Too Big To Fail

Too Big To Fail refers to the disturbing but proven concept that some businesses have become so enormous and systemically important that the jurisdictional government has no choice but to save them from failing with whatever means necessary. The governments feel they must deliver material assistance to the firms in order to prevent a catastrophic rogue wave effect from reverberating across the entire economy.

The simple explanation for how a company can be so important to an entire economy is this. When such an enormous firm fails, all of the companies that count on it for parts of their revenue can also be compromised and fail, as well as its debt holders and ancillary services providing companies that work with the failing massive firm. Jobs then become eliminated en masse. For this reason, the expenses involved with a simple bailout or government backed guarantees of the mega corporation are significantly less than the cost of overall widespread economic failures. It explains why governments will often opt for the bailout as the less expensive answer to the moral problem.

Too Big To Fail especially pertains to commercial banks and financial services firms. These financial companies are so critical for the United States' and other Western economies that it would create havoc and spread financial ruin if they declared bankruptcy. Because of this, the American and British governments especially opted in the Global Financial Crisis of 2008-2009 to spare the banks and other financial service firms.

They saved the bank creditors and holders of counter party risk. As an unwished for side effect, they allowed the managers and company board members to keep their enormous salaries and incredible bonuses. Throughout the last years of the 2000's, the United States' Federal Government doled out approximately $700 billion in order to shore up such critical failing corporations as Bear Stearns, AIG, and the major banks which stood on the edge of financial ruin.

It was investors' total evaporation in confidence of the major financial institutions that led to their near-downfall back in the years 2008 and 2009. Especially the investment banks ran into trouble as they had become unbelievably leveraged (to the tune of from forty to one and eighty to one) when suddenly their mortgage loan-based assets and derivatives plunged in value as the subprime mortgage crisis spiraled out of control. Both stake holders and creditors quickly began to have doubts in their financial solvency as their balance sheets crumbled.

The defining moment in the Too Big To Fail crisis erupted when the government did not step in to prevent Lehman Brothers investment bank from failing. This has become widely known as the "Lehman moment." As widespread chaos erupted in the financial markets, regulators suddenly became painfully aware that these largest companies were so intricately connected that it would take enormous financial bailouts in order to stop literally half of the U.S. financial sector from collapsing.

Once the bailouts had intervened to save the major Too Big To Fail investment banks, only two remained standing. Even the survivors Morgan Stanley and Goldman Sachs were both forced to convert to traditional commercial banks so that they could be backstopped by the FDIC. Bear Stearns was effectively wound down, Lehman's skeleton was bought out by Barclays of Great Britain, and once-mighty Merrill Lynch became a subsidiary of Bank of America. The shadow banking industry had all but disappeared overnight.

The government then attempted to address the issues of Too Big To Fail financial firms. The U.S. Congress passed the Dodd-Frank Wall Street Reform and Consumer Protection Act of 2010. The idea was to create restrictions which would make it far more difficult for such conditions to flourish again. They hoped to sidestep having to extend other bailouts in the future.

The Act made the financial institutions create forms of "living wills" so that their plans are in place in order to rapidly liquidate assets if they have to file for bankruptcy. An internationally based consortium of financial regulators came up with a new set of rules in November of 2015 to force the major global banks to raise their capital by $1.2 trillion more in additional debt funding which they are able to convert into equity or write off if they suffer catastrophic losses again.

Toxic Assets

Toxic Assets is a coined phrase for those financial assets which saw their actual value plummet. Toxic assets do not have well working markets anymore, making them difficult or impossible to sell for a price on which the owner will agree. The term arose as a popularly coined phrase during the financial crisis of 2007-2010. Toxic assets proved to have a major part in causing the financial crisis.

As toxic assets' markets seize up, they are called frozen markets. Many markets for these toxic assets froze up starting in 2007. The problem only continued to grow exponentially worse in the second half of the following year 2008. A number of elements combined to lock up the markets for toxic assets. These assets had values that proved to be extremely vulnerable to the worsening economic situation. As uncertainty only grew in this scenario, finding a value for toxic assets became more difficult. In the resulting frozen markets, banks and similar lending institutions chose not to unload these assets for greatly diminished prices. The reason for it lay in their fear that such drastically lower prices would force them to mark down all of their holdings, so that they became insolvent or bankrupt.

Typically, toxic assets are able to clear when the supply and demand of them reach the point that buyers and sellers will come together. This did not occur in the financial crisis starting in 2007. As a number of the financial assets simply hung around on banks' balance sheets, experts declared that the markets had broken down.

Another way of putting this is that because banks would not write down the prices on the assets, the price of them proved to be overly high. Buyers knew that these assets were now worth far less than the selling banks hoped to realize for them. This kept the sellers' price expectations far higher than buyers were willing to pay.

Toxic assets mostly arose as a result of banks and other investment banks deciding to pour enormous sums of money into new and complex financial assets like credit default swaps and collateralized debt obligations. These highly leveraged assets had values that turned out to be extremely vulnerable to a variety of economic conditions like the rates of default, prices of houses, and liquidity of financial markets. These toxic assets threatened to destroy the entire financial system and did manage to take down a number of venerable institutions like Bear Stearns, Lehman Brothers, and Washington Mutual Bank, the country's largest savings and loan institution. As a result of the carnage created by these highly leveraged, speculative investments in toxic assets, experts have named them financial weapons of mass destruction.

Tranches

Tranches refer to a French word that means a portion or a slice. In the world of investing, it relates to securities which may be subdivided into tinier parts and then sold off to various interested investors. These securities typically represent structured financing. Every part of the tranche is a portion of a few correlated securities that specific banks called investment banks offer all at once. Yet each of the tranches comes with its own set of rewards, risks, and maturities.

MBS Mortgage backed securities are often represented in tranches. There are different types of these MBS. One of them is the CMO collateralized mortgage obligation. Such securities will be subdivided up according to their maturity dates. At this point, the offering firm will sell them to investors who buy them according to the maturity date they prefer. Looking at an example helps to clarify the concept as it pertains to CMOs. An investment bank might offer a tranche or several of them made up of mortgages. The maturity dates on these could vary according to twenty year, ten year, five year, two year, and single year maturities. Each of these would offer a range of returns versus risks. Every maturity would be its own tranche in this example.

There are particular reasons why various investors would prefer different types. In one scenario, the investors might require shorter term cash flows yet not wish to have any in the longer term future. Still other investors might wish for longer term cash flow but not need it today. Because of these different needs from investors, investment banks might decide to split up their assets in the CMOs. They could assign them to different parts, or tranches. This way the former investor is able to obtain his initial cash flow from an underlying group of mortgages while the latter investor can obtain the later period cash flows. Thanks to the investment banks forming such tranches, the CMO securities which might not have attracted sufficient investor interest can acquire a new lease on life through a variety of investors with different needs.

Tranches find a great deal of use in numerous mortgage pools which contain many different types of mortgages. There would usually be riskier loans in the pool that came with greater interest rates. At the same time, more conservative loans that come with lower interest rates will be in most pools. Every pool of mortgages will also possess its own maturity dates that bear on the reward to risk ratios. This is why the investment banks create these tranches into smaller pieces which each contain their own particular common set of financial characteristics that appeal to certain investor scenarios. For any investors who desire to put their capital to work in MBOs, they are able to select the specific tranche kind that will best suit their level of risk tolerance as well as their hoped- for return.

Each of the tranches gets its ultimate value from the mortgage pools which underlie them. The investors who purchase these MBOs are allowed to hold them for longer term, smaller gains that come from the interest payments. They might also decide to attempt to sell them early on for a rapid profit. It is also possible to pursue a combination of strategies, trying to obtain slower steady income for a certain amount of time before selling them off at a profit.

The monthly payments come from pieces of the total interest payments mortgage holders make each month (to their mortgage holder) within the given tranche. This is why those investors who purchase them will obtain a monthly cash flow from the specific MBO tranche in which they invest, so long as they hold on to the tranche.

Transfer of Interest

A Transfer of Interest refers to an individual, business, or other organization choosing to transfer over its ownership in an asset or object. This could be a business entity, piece of Real Estate, or asset that the owner shifts to another party. Most commonly the term becomes utilized regarding the transferring of an entity's ownership of an interest in a business. This could involve transfers between parties in a limited liability company, a partnership, a privately held sole proprietorship, or even a corporation. In the vast majority of cases, such a transfer occurs with a contract known as a transfer of interest agreement.

In theory, any time individuals or businesses engage in a purchase, they are becoming party to a contract. Such contracts are actually making a Transfer of Interest in some form of real property in the vast majority of cases. As a concrete example, when an individual buys food off of a supermarket or produce stand, this literally represents an implied contract (evidenced by a receipt as proof of purchase). The end result is that the buyer becomes the transferring new owner of the food purchase. The same is true when people buy clothing from a department store. The ownership of the clothes becomes officially transferred by the contract which the store makes with the buyer when money changes hands in exchange for a receipt and the articles of clothing.

Any type of Transfer of Interest is affected with whatever terms the two parties agree upon at the time of transfer. These could involve legal restrictions and stipulations on the kind of interest which they will transfer between them. The appropriate agreement only has to state clearly the interest which will be transferred, the parties who are involved, and the sum being delivered in consideration of the interest transfer. After the transaction intent is clearly stated by the actions and/or verbal promises of the two parties in question, the agreement will be officially concluded so that the transfer becomes finalized.

Naturally the universe of Real Estate has its own highly evolved and carefully developed procedures for such an important Transfer of Interest. They commonly call this an assessable transfer of interest. It refers to the reality of taxation which goes along with tangible interest in and de facto ownership of Real Estate. These transfers mandate that the property will be appraised and fully re-evaluated in the tax year that follows the transfer. All transfers of Real Estate done either with a contract, trust, or deed will be treated as such by the taxing authorities in the relevant jurisdiction. Leases that last for more than 20 years also come under this requirement. The reason for such an evaluation of the property value is to be certain that the taxes are fairly and fully assessed on the Real Estate involved in the contractual transfer transaction.

It is many times the same when there is a Transfer of Interest in a business accomplished through a sale. This event often produces an assessable event which will require a tax assessment to be done. When the business is at least 50 percent sold, this will commonly be required. When a business is instead forfeited or foreclosed on and the change of status does not lead to an income tax event, then this is an exception to the tax assessment rule.

When a transfer occurs among an affiliated group's members, this is also an applicable exception to the assessment case. There are often these substantial tax ramifications to such a transfer of a business that the government will usually require that the business value be reassessed following the execution of the business transfer transaction in question.

Trust

A Trust proves to be a special type of fiduciary arrangement where one participant the trustor grants the other participant the trustee the rights to possess the property title or assets title for the advantages of the beneficiary, often times a third party. When it is utilized in the world of finance, this similarly refers to a kind of closed end investment fund collectively established as a public limited company.

Settlors ultimately establish such trusts. They elect to shift over all or a portion of their possessions (assets) to the trustees of the trust in this action. It is the trustees who ultimately maintain the assets on behalf of the beneficiaries of said trust. The trusts' rules come down to the particular terms that apply to the given trust in question. Some jurisdictions allow for older members of the beneficiaries' class to ascend to the roles of trustee. Some of these jurisdictions actually allow for the grantor to be both a trustee and lifetime beneficiary together at once.

Two different types of trusts exist, the testamentary trust and the living trust. The testamentary trusts are also known as will trusts. These determine the means in which the assets for the individuals will be allocated after they eventually pass away. The document of such a trust comes into play legally following the death of the testator.

On the other hand, living trusts are known as inter vivos or revocable trusts. These written out documents allow for the assets of an individual to be created in the form of a trust. The individual himself or a beneficiary will then enjoy the advantages of and utilization of the resources throughout their remaining lives. Such assets will eventually be transferred to the legal beneficiaries when the individual dies. The trust creator sets a successor trustee who will carry the responsibility of transferring any remaining assets over to the beneficiary in question.

There are a number of different reasons that individuals employ trusts. One of these is to attain a degree of privacy. Wills and their arrangements are often public domain material in many jurisdictions. Trusts can specify the identical conditions which a will may, without the intrusive nature of being public domain documents available for any and all members of the public to read upon demand. This explains why those people who do not wish to have their wills and terms of their estate disposition revealed publically after they are gone will often choose to utilize trusts for their final bequests instead of the will document.

Besides this, trusts are a useful vehicle for planning the payment of taxes. Trusts have different tax arrangements than do standard planning accounts and competing vehicles. The tax consequences for deploying such trusts are typically less negative and expensive than those of other typical means involved in financial planning. This helps to explain why using trusts has become a standard option in the world of efficient tax planning. This is the case not only for individuals but also for corporations.

Finally, trusts find extensive utilization in estate planning procedures. This allows for the assets of deceased people to be passed on to their spouses. The spouses are then able to equally divide up the remaining assets for the benefit of the children who survive the deceased parent. Those children who do not possess the necessary 18 years of age to be considered legal persons (with possession rights) will be required to have trustees to exercise control over all assets in question until they reach the legal age of adulthood.

Trust Account

A trust account refers to a type of account which a trustee holds on the behalf of the beneficiary. The trustee does not have the ability to utilize the funds in any personal capacity, but merely to safe keep, disburse, and invest them for the advantage of the beneficiary.

An example of this type of arrangement is when an attorney holds funds for the benefit of the client. The attorney will not be able to draw upon the funds until after a certain protocol takes place. As the attorney earns the lawyer fees, the client will have to first review and then actually approve the bill from the attorney before he or she can transfer the client funds from this trust account over to the general account of the attorney for settlement of bills.

There are a number of reasons and situations in which individuals may opt to establish a trust account. In some scenarios, people wish to disperse a pre-determined sum of money to their family or other loved ones over a number of years or throughout the remainder of their natural lives.

As a real world example, consider the following. Parents may wish to establish some trust accounts which will provide money to their dependents and/or children every month if and when they die. In such a scenario, it would normally be banking brokers who would manage such accounts. In fact these broker trustees would draw down the account values by the appropriate amount every month or year as they disbursed the either monthly or yearly funds to the beneficiaries for the individuals who originally formed the trust.

There are other common kinds of trusts as well. One of these is a property tax trust account. Such accounts will be established by entrepreneurs of real estate who own a variety of properties. Rather than have to be concerned about the property tax funds and disbursements to the appropriate taxing authorities themselves, they elect to form a trust account which will pay the taxes. This prevents the entrepreneurs from forfeiting their valuable properties because they forgot to pay the property taxes. There are a number of monetary benefits to having such an account. One of these is that estate taxes will not apply to properties contained in such a trust when the owner dies.

There are two different main types of trust accounts. These are revocable and irrevocable trusts. With revocable trusts, these represent deposit accounts whose owners chose to name one or several beneficiaries. These beneficiaries would then obtain the deposits in the account once the holder of the account died. As the name implies, such revocable trusts may be terminated, revoked, or altered on demand whenever the holder of said account wishes. In this particular case, the owner is the trustor, settlor, or grantor of the revocable trust in question. These types of trusts will be established as either informal or formal. While trustees are powerful and have a broad scope of authority over the assets of the beneficiary, they are not omnipotent, but must be bound by the laws and regulations of the jurisdiction which pertain to trust accounts.

Irrevocable trusts on the other hand are similarly deposit accounts but they are not titled in the name of the owner. Instead these become titled as an irrevocable trust for the name. The owner, trustor, settlor, or grantor also makes deposits of money or other valuable assets to the trust account. The principal difference is that the owners forfeit all ability to alter or cancel the trust once they have established it. These types of trusts also become created once an owner of a revocable type of trust dies. They can be set up through a judicial order as well, or even by a statute as appropriate.

Trustee

Trustee refers to either a firm or an individual who possesses assets or real estate property on behalf of a third party individual, group, or organization. Trustees are often appointed to perform a great range of functions. These could be for charities, bankruptcies, trust funds, pension plans, or retirement plans.

As the name implies, these individuals or firms are entrusted with taking the optimal decisions which are in the primary interest of the beneficiary. Because of this sacred trust, these are often considered to be fiduciary responsibilities for the beneficiary or beneficiaries of the trust in question. This means that they are legally bound and obligated to perform these duties to the very best of their capabilities.

The granting of the prestigious title and responsibilities of trustee comes in the form of a legal title bestowed by a trust. Trusts themselves prove to be legal arrangements which two willingly consenting parties agree to make. Because of the fiduciary nature of the trustee role in any trust which the individual or organization oversees for the beneficiary or beneficiaries, they must lay aside any and all hopes of individual gain or personal agendas so that they can perform the best actions on behalf of the trust.

In other words, the trustee carries the full responsibility for correctly and optimally managing both the financial assets and real estate types of property which the trust itself possesses. There will always be duties particular to the specific details of the trust which the trustees must perform. The differing types of assets will naturally dictate the activities which the trustees must engage in for the beneficiaries' common good.

It helps to consider a real world example to more fully understand the somewhat complex concept. When trusts are made up of a range of real estate properties, the trustees will be responsible for properly overseeing the maintenance and handling of the particular pieces of property. In other cases, a trust might be comprised of different investments such as stocks, mutual funds, and bond holdings in a stock brokerage firm account. The trustees in this case will have to properly oversee and mange as necessary the account or accounts for the beneficiaries.

Trustees also have certain guidelines to which they must adhere in general. Among these common responsibilities which pertain no matter what the particulars of the trust agreement may actually be, the assets must be at all times kept under the direct control of the trustees so that they are securely accounted for each and every day. Trustees also must fully grasp the often unique terms of their particular trust, the responsibilities they are incurring by taking on the role, and the wishes of the applicable beneficiaries. Assets which may be invested must be considered productive so that they will benefit the beneficiary or beneficiaries in the future.

Besides this, the trustees have to both understand and properly interpret the trust arrangement so that they can effectively administer the assets' distribution to the correct parties and/or beneficiaries. This includes the duties of compiling all appropriate records for the trust. Among these there will be tax returns which they must file and pay and statements that they must produce and deliver to the beneficiaries. As such, the trustees will be expected to maintain regular communication with all beneficiaries so that they remain informed of the value of related accounts and any taxes which will become due.

In the end, all trustees have the distinction of being the ultimate decision makers regarding every trust-related matter. They must make such decisions according to the particular provisions contained within their unique trust arrangement and contract. It also means that if beneficiaries have questions regarding a decision which the trustee is preparing to take, that they must first obtain answers for these beneficiaries before they engage in the given decision.

Underwriting

Underwriting refers to a means of determining if a consumer is eligible or not for a particular kind of financial product. These products vary depending on the person's or business' requirements. They might include home mortgages, insurance coverage needs, business mortgages, lines of credit, or financing for venture start up projects. The bank or other financial institution undergoing the underwriting evaluation procedure will look into the odds of the business transaction successfully providing them with a profit in exchange for their offer of financial help.

As banks and insurance firms go through the underwriting process, two different things will occur. The first of these is showing an interest in the project that the borrower is proposing for finance. They demonstrate this by offering the financial aid that the customer is requesting. Next, with a bank or institution underwriting an insurance policy, residential or commercial mortgage, or venture, they are looking to make money on their investment one day in the future. They might either gather these profits at one time in the form of a lump sum at a future date or little by little in monthly payments. In these underwriting activities, compensation is expected, which is commonly paid via finance charges or other fees.

Underwriters contemplate more than simply the amount of risk that an applicant demonstrates. They also consider the potential risk that working with the new customer might bring to other customers of their company. In order to ensure that the bank or firm does not suffer too much harm to keep up with commitments made to already existing clients, they have developed underwriting standards.

Insurance companies heavily rely on underwriting in performing their business. Health insurance is one example of this. Health insurance providers seriously look into the past and present health of a person applying. Sometimes their underwriting will show that they need to exclude various pre-existing conditions for a certain amount of time when they insure the person. Other times, underwriting will reveal a medical history that demonstrates too much risk for the company. In this case, a health insurance company will refuse to provide the requested health insurance coverage. Their goal is to not insure individuals who they believe will need significant medical treatment over time, so that they can provide a solid financial backing for their existing clientele.

In business, underwriting is commonly employed to determine if new ventures should be given financing. An example of this might be a company that has created a new technology that it wishes to sell. These underwriters will consider how marketable the product appears, the applicant's marketing plan, the expense of creating and selling the new items, and also the odds of the company realizing profits on every piece that they sell. Sometimes, underwriters of these business ventures will express an interest in having shares of stock in the start up company as a portion of their payment for services. Other times, they will only require a set interest rate for the dollar amount invested.

UniCredit Bulbank

UniCredit Bulbank proves to be the biggest bank in the Republic of Bulgaria. Until 1994, this state-controlled and -operated bank bore the name of the Bulgarian Foreign Trade Bank or BFTB. It was in 2007 that the UniCredit Bulbank became formed when Bulbank, Hebros Bank, and Biochim merged together as individual subsidiaries of UniCredit Group from Italy.

Bulgarian Foreign Trade Bank first arose in 1964 in its headquarters of Sofia, Bulgaria. The at the time completely state-owned and -founded bank held an initial paid in capital of 40 million Bulgarian leva when it opened. This proved to be a large sum of capital in this day and age. At the time under the heyday of the communists in Bulgaria it specialized in foreign finance and foreign trade payments.

The bank realized that to effectively pursue foreign trade and finance, it needed several well placed good international branches. The bank then began to open important representative offices in London, Vienna, and Frankfurt throughout the subsequent decades. In 2015, the operation boasted substantially greater assets amounting to nearly 9 billion Euros and 2015 era equity of nearly 13 billion Euros.

Once Communism collapsed in Bulgaria during the successful national coup in 1989, the country established the Bank Consolidation Company in 1991 to operate the state- controlled banking sector and to help with the eventual privatizing of the various national Bulgarian banks. BCC owned 98 percent of the share capital of Bulbank at the time. It became the first Bulgarian bank operation to change over to international SWIFT codes. This helped it to massively improve its transaction reliability and operational performance as a direct result.

The bank's eventual privatization from 1998 to 2000 saw UniCredito Italiano gain control of 93 percent of the capital shares while German based re-insurance giant Allianz obtained another five percent of the remaining shares. Bulbank then sold its majority stakes in Corporate Commercial Bank and minor stakes in United Bulgarian Bank and HypoVereinsbank Bulgaria.

Bulbank has continuously worked on the merger of operations and branches between the old Bulbank offices and Hebros Bank and HVB Bank Biochim since UniCredit made the decision to merge the HVB Group back in 2005. The group was renamed UniCredit Bulbank officially at this point.

The same Chief Executive Officer has overseen the company's massive successes since the year 2001. This towering figure in Bulgarian banking and finance is Mr. Levon Hampartzoumian. He heads UniCredit Bulbank still as of end of 2016 in its second decade of existence in the present foreign owned-form of the financial institution.

Part of the leading in Bulgaria success that UniCredit Bulbank has consistently enjoyed in recent decades stems from the wide range of clientele they effectively serve. They offer bank checking, current, and savings accounts, insurance and investment products, land and home mortgages, and financing and credit for individual clients, private banking customers, small businesses, large corporate clients, other financial institutions, and even Bulgarian government and other public institutions as well.

UniCredit Bulbank is not only by far and away the largest bank in Bulgaria by branches, deposits, and assets; it is also a heavily award-winning financial institution. In 2016, it received the honors of "Bank of the Year" from the Association Bank of the Year and "Best Bank for 2016" from Global Finance Magazine. It is known as the "Best Digital Bank in Bulgaria for 2016" per Global Finance Magazine. Focus Economics ranks it as the "Most Precise Overall Economic Forecast for Bulgaria." Forbes Magazine labeled it the "Most Innovative Bank in Bulgaria". It received the "Best Bank in Bulgaria" designations from EMEA Finance Magazine and K10's Kapital Newspaper annual ranking. Global Finance Magazine called UniCredit Bulbank the "Best Trade Finance Bank in Bulgaria" in 2016, as did Euromoney Magazine as well.

Vacancy Rate

Vacancy rates turn out to be statistics that are gathered and maintained on availability of homes for sale, rental properties, and hotels. When you see high rates of vacancy, this is evidence that a market is struggling. Lower vacancy rates are hoped for as they demonstrate that properties are in demand and vacancies do not stay open for much time. Government agencies and other companies that focus on economic analysis maintain the records on vacancy rates. If you are contemplating moving into a new community, then you will find that vacancy rates are worth contemplating.

Where housing is concerned, vacancy rates add up all housing units that can be lived in but are not presently occupied. The agencies compiling the vacancy rates then express this as the percent of available to be lived in housing that is presently vacant. Vacancy rates cover houses, townhouses, apartments, and other forms of housing. As vacancy rates prove to be lower, it becomes more difficult for individuals to obtain housing. This is because the types of housing that they want may not be available either for sale or rent on a regular basis.

The vacancy rate statistics can be found on various kinds of housing arrangements. This differentiates on vacancy rates between townhouses, apartments, and single family homes. Landlords read these vacancy rates to be appraised of the rental situation, since changes in this number impact how much rent they can charge tenants. If landlords' tenants are constantly leaving, causing high rates of turnover, then they may wrestle with high vacancy rates personally.

When you see high vacancy rates in housing, it indicates that economic recession or depression is evident. High rates of vacancy can also happen if a great number of individuals leave a particular community, causing significant quantities of homes to lie vacant. Developers incorrectly estimating how strong a market is for housing in a local community might also cause them. Another factor that leads to higher vacancy rates proves to be rents that are high. When individuals can not pay an area's rent, then they will look for other places to live. Hotel vacancy rates demonstrate the strength or weakness of an area economy more profoundly, since high hotel vacancies mean tourism in the area is down.

Businesses are concerned with commercial vacancy rates. These are commonly figured up separate from residential vacancies. In the business vacancy rates figure are commercial buildings like factories and warehouses, and also empty retail storefronts and offices. Lower rates mean that people are supporting the businesses by spending their dollars in those areas. When consumers see a large number of empty storefronts, even when the economy is doing well, it will discourage them from frequenting that plaza or area.

Any individual who wants to see the vacancy rates for a given community can get them. A good place to start looking is at a local government office and in census data. Besides this, Realtors commonly maintain statistics on area vacancy rates, as do Internet sites that keep demographic information on different communities.

Wealth

Wealth proves to be the abundant possession of material things or other resources that are considered to be valuable. People, areas, communities, or nations who control these assets are said to be wealthy. The word for wealth comes from the old English word 'Weal' and 'th', which means 'the conditions of well-being'.

The ideas of wealth have great importance for every part of the study of economics. This is particularly the case with development economics. Since the definition of wealth often depends on the situation in which you use it, no universally accepted definition for wealth exists. Different individuals have expressed a number of varying ideas of wealth in differing scenarios. Stating the concept of wealth often involves ethics and moral issues, because the accumulation of wealth is viewed by many people as the highest goal.

Wealth is not evenly distributed throughout the world. In the year 2000, world wealth estimates ranged around $125 trillion. The citizens of Europe, North America, and a few high income Asian countries have ninety percent of all of this wealth. Besides this shocking statistic, only one percent of all adults on earth possess forty percent of the planet's wealth. This number declines to thirty-two percent when wealth is calculated according to purchasing power parity, or equivalency of what it buys from one country to the next.

Wealth and richness are two separate words that are used interchangeably. They mean slightly different things. Wealth describes gathering up resources, whether they are common or abundant. Richness relates to having such resources in abundance. Wealthy countries and people possess many more resources than do poor ones. The word richness is similarly employed to describe peoples' basic needs being fulfilled through sharing the collective abundance. Wealth's opposite proves to be destitution, while richness' opposite is known as poverty.

It is a concept that requires a social contract of ownership to be set up and enforced. Ideas of wealth are actually relative. They range from not only one society and people to another, but even between varying regions or areas of the same society or nation. As an example, having ten thousand dollars throughout all of the United States does not make a person among the richest in any area of the country. But this amount in desperately poor developing nations would represent a huge quantity of wealth.

The idea of wealth changes in different times too. Thanks to the progress of science and machines that save labor, even the poorest in America today benefit from a higher standard of living than the wealthy used to enjoy not so long ago. Assuming this trend continues, then the wealthiest people's standard of living today will be considered poor in the future.

Wire Transfer

A wire transfer is the quickest, safest, most reliable means of sending money within the United States, in other countries, or around the world. They are often essential in the more critical financial activities of life such as purchasing a house. The reason larger transactions occur in this form of payment is because the recipient can receive and verify the funds transfer the same day it is done, or as near to immediately as possible (besides Western Union and Money Gram, which cost substantially more to utilize).

A wire transfer actually represents a means to electronically transfer money from one party to another via a bank as intermediary. A traditional and typical wire transfer starts at a credit union or bank and electronically processes through either Fedwire or SWIFT networks. Another common name for such a wire transfer is a bank wire, which also encompasses the standard bank to bank transfers.

Ultimately the wire transfers have become so successful and utilized throughout the United States and rest of world simply because they are capable of moving even enormous sums of money to any destination bank in the world in only a day or two. If they are affected within the same country such as the United States then same day wires can be done. For an international transfer via wire transfer, it often requires another day or even two to complete.

Since the funds move rapidly through the financial system, recipients are not required to wait a material amount of time for the funds to become cleared. This means they can access and utilize the money without significant delays. No holds are typically placed on wire transfer monies. The safety issue means that merchants prefer the wire mechanism. This is because checks can bounce because of insufficient funds, while wires never do so. In other words, these are guaranteed funds.

There are some particular requirements that wire transfers need in order to be possible to transact. At least in the United States, both parties would require a functioning bank account in order for a bank to act as intermediary. Since thieves can not open a bank account too easily, nor bank anonymously in the United States, it is difficult for them to carry out scams using bank wires. This is because it leaves a paper trail which is easy for law enforcement officials to follow.

This does not mean that wire transfer scams are unknown entirely. It is possible for a person to be tricked into wiring money to a fraudster for a purchase or service they never receive. Examples of this are fake insurance policies or false retirement or investment products. Once the wire has cleared the recipients account, they can either withdraw the funds in person or wire it to an offshore overseas account.

By the time the victims realize that they have been scammed, the funds sent by wire will be long gone. They would no longer be recoverable by traditional U.S. law enforcement or even court order methods once they have been transferred offshore. Pulling money back after it has been dispatched via bank wire is extremely difficult in any case. This is true even if the funds remain in the recipient's bank account.

Wire transfer fees can be significant. In many parts of the United States, they run as high as $40 to dispatch a bank wire. Many banks charge upwards of $10 in order for a bank wire to be received into an account. The costs to send one are higher if the wire is funded by utilizing a credit card cash advance. Cash advance fees would then apply, as well as typically large interest rates, plus the wire transfer fee. This is why it is typically most financially sound to effect a bank wire directly from the sender's bank account.

Zoning Laws

Zoning laws are statutes that mandate the ways that you are able to utilize your property holdings. Townships, counties, cities, and alternative local governments affect zoning laws so that they are able to create standards for development that benefit all residents in common.

It does not matter how big or how small a property is; it will be impacted by zoning laws. If you contemplate improving your property or purchasing another piece of property, you should be certain that you are fully aware of zoning restrictions that will affect you in advance of making any kind of commitment.

As an example, properties can be zoned according to residential or commercial restrictions. Commercial buildings will never be permitted to be constructed in a residential area, while residential dwellings can not be put up in commercial zones, unless the zoning laws of the area are changed.

Getting the zoning laws for a property altered proves to be extremely difficult. You would first have to give out public notice before getting an approved variance from the responsible government agencies in charge of zoning plans. Many times, neighbors will stalwartly resist your proposed zoning changes.

Zoning laws allow for a variety of different zoning designations and uses. Among these are commercial zoning, residential zoning, industrial zoning, recreational zoning, and agricultural zoning. These categories are generally further subdivided into other categories. Residential zoning might have sub zoning categories under it including multiple family use, for condominiums or apartments, or single family houses.

Zoning laws include a number of limitations to the property and potential improvements. The total size and height of buildings on the property is commonly restricted. The buildings can only be placed so close to each other. There will be limits to the total area percentage that is allowed to have buildings on it. Perhaps most importantly, the types of buildings that can be built on a given land's zone will be mandated.

You can learn about the zoning laws and ordinances simply by getting in touch with the area planning agency. Alternatively, you might go on the Internet to the local and state search engine to learn about your county and city zoning rules. Local planning organizations will tell you what must be done to get a variance to the area zoning.

Other Financial Books by Thomas Herold

Herold Financial IQ Series
Financial Education Is Your Best Investment

Get Smart with the Financial IQ Series

The Herold Financial IQ series covers all major areas and aspects of the financial world. Starting with Personal Finance, Real Estate and Banking term. Covering Corporate Finance, Investment as well as Economics.

It also includes Retirement, Trading, and Accounting terms. In addition, you'll find Debt, Bankruptcy, Mortgage, Small Business, and Wall Street terminology explained. Not to forget Laws & Regulations as well as important acronyms and abbreviations.

Available on Amazon as Kindle, Paperback and Audio Edition

Go to Amazon.com and search for 'Herold Financial IQ' or copy and paste this link below.

http://bit.ly/herold-financial-iq

High Credit Score Secrets - The Smart Raise And Repair Guide to Excellent Credit

Poor Credit Score Could Cost You Hundreds of Thousands of Dollars
A recent financial statistic revealed that increasing your score from 'fair' to 'good' saves you an average of $86,200* over a lifetime. Imagine what you could do with that extra money?

Improve Your Credit Score in 45-60 Days or Even Less
This practical credit compendium starts off by demonstrating over 50 guaranteed methods of how you can almost immediately boost your credit score. Follow these simple, effective and proven strategies to improve your credit score from as low as 450 points to over 810.

Don't let bad credit hold you back from achieving financial freedom. Your credit score not only influences all your future choices, but it also can save you thousands of dollars.

Available on Amazon as Kindle, Paperback and Audio Edition
Go to Amazon.com and search for 'High Credit Score Secrets' or copy and paste this link below.

http://bit.ly/high-credit

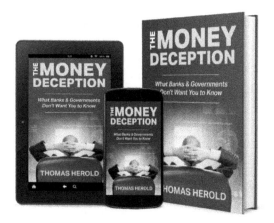

The Money Deception
What Banks & Governments Don't Want You to Know

„It is well enough that people of the nation do not understand our banking and monetary system, for if they did, I believe there would be a revolution before tomorrow morning." - Henry Ford

The Catastrophic Results of Money Manipulation
This money has been souped up by the 1% that now controls 50% of the world's wealth. The fastest and biggest wealth transfer in history is underway. Money evaporates from the middle class, leaving them struggling and without hope for retirement.

What's Happening to Your Money?
Going all the way down into the rabbit hole, it shows you the root of the problem and also lays the foundation for the future. It describes the most likely transition into a new worldwide crypto-based currency, which will become the new basis of our financial system.

Available on Amazon as Kindle, Paperback and Audio Edition
Go to Amazon.com and search for 'Money Deception' or copy and paste this link below.

http://bit.ly/money-deception

Other Books in the Herold Financial IQ Series

99 Financial Terms Every Beginner, Entrepreneur & Business Should Know

Personal Finance Terms

Real Estate Terms

Bank & Banking Terms

Corporate Finance Terms

Investment Terms

Economics Terms

Retirement Terms

Stock Trading Terms

Accounting Terms

Debt & Bankruptcy Terms

Mortgage Terms

Small Business Terms

Wall Street Terms

Laws & Regulations

Financial Acronyms